BRIJESH RAWAT

First Published in July 2022

ISBN: 978-93-5628-800-3

BLUEROSE PUBLISHERS

www.BlueRoseONE.com

info@bluerosepublishers.com

+91 8882 898 898

Cover Design:

Aman Sharma

Typographic Design:

Namrata Saini

Distributed by: BlueRose, Amazon, Flipkart

This book is dedicated to my family

They do not want to be named

&

All the Old boys of Mayo College,

THEY COULDN'T CARE LESS

Preface

With the onset of the Corona Pandemic. Finding myself totally idle, we the boys of the batch of 1968, from Mayo College, Ajmer, formed a Whatsapp group, primarily to share Jokes and other humorous incidents,

This is the result, so I am printing it to share with the world.

Acknowledgements

The author hereby acknowledges that all this compilation is from the humor circulating in social media, and none of this is the author's original work.

Intellectual's Humour

Dr Sarvapalli Radhakrishnan, a great Teacher, Philosopher and former President of India in whose honour Teachers' Day is celebrated, was an exceptionally "witty man"..!!

The King of Greece came to India on a State visit.

President Radhakrishnan welcomed him at the Palam Airport.

"Your Majesty... You are the first King of Greece to come to India "on invitation..."!!

The last time, Alexander, the Great, "came uninvited."

****

Gandhiji: Don't drink Milk which is the essence of Beef.

Radhakrishnan: "In that case, we all are Cannibals. For, we drink our Mother's Milk, which again is the essence of Human Flesh."

****

Winston Churchill while having a cup of Tea said to Dr. Radhakrishnan:
Sugar is the only English word where "s" is pronounced as "sh"..!!

Dr.quipped: "Are you sure?"

Once Winston Churchill hosted a State Banquet in honour of Dr Radhakrishnan who washed his hands before eating and used his hands for having the food while Churchill used Spoons and Forks..!!

Churchill could not stop himself from advising Dr.Radhakrishnan to use Spoon and Fork saying that they were more hygienic.

☞ Radhakrishnan replied...“
Since nobody can use my hand to eat, my hand is more hygienic than any Spoon or Fork you use”..!!☺☺

****

On one of his travels abroad, Dr.Sarvapalli Radhakrishnan was asked a question by a member in the audience.

"What's the difference between a Station Master and a School Master...!"

The question was irrelevant and bordering on impertinent, too..!!
However, this brilliant gentleman replied calmly...
"While a Station Master minds the Train, a School Master trains the mind...!" ☺👍

****

Saturday morning I got up early, quietly dressed, made my lunch, and slipped quietly into the garage. I hooked up the boat up to the van and proceeded to back out into a torrential downpour. The wind was blowing 50mph, so I pulled back into the garage, turned on the radio, and discovered that the weather would be bad all day.

I went back into the house, quietly undressed, and slipped back into bed. I cuddled up to my wife's back; now with a different anticipation, and whispered, "The weather out there is terrible."

My loving wife of 5 years replied, "And, can you believe my husband is out fishing in that?"

****

After retiring, I went to the Social Security office to apply for Social Security.

The woman behind the counter asked me for my driver's License to verify my age. I looked in my pockets and realized I had left my wallet at home. I told the woman that I was very sorry, but I would have to go home and come back later.

The woman said, 'Unbutton your shirt'. So I opened my shirt revealing my curly silver hair.

She said, 'That silver hair on your chest is proof enough for me' and she processed my Social Security application.

When I got home, I excitedly told my wife about my experience at

The Social Security office. She said, 'You should have dropped your pants. You might have gotten disability too.'

My wife was standing nude, looking in the bedroom mirror. She was not happy with what she saw and said to me,

"I feel horrible; I look old, fat and ugly. I really need you to pay me a compliment.'

I replied, "Your eyesight's damn near perfect."

And then the fight started........

****

I rear-ended a car this morning...the start of a REALLY bad day!

The driver got out of the other car, and he was a DWARF!!

He looked up at me and said 'I am NOT Happy!'

So I said, 'Well, which one ARE you then?'

That's how the fight started.

****

This is a very powerful and moving story. Don't read it too fast. Enjoy!

YOU REAP WHAT YOU SOW

Good morning said a woman as she walked up to the man sitting on the ground.

The man slowly looked up.

This was a woman clearly accustomed to the finer things of life. Her coat was new. She looked like she had never missed a meal in her life.

His first thought was that she wanted to make fun of him, like so many others had done before. "Leave me alone," he growled....

To his amazement, the woman continued standing.

She was smiling -- her even white teeth displayed in dazzling rows. "Are you hungry?" she asked.

"No," he answered sarcastically. "I've just come from dining with the president. Now go away."

The woman's smile became even broader. Suddenly the man felt a gentle hand under his arm.

"What are you doing, lady?" the man asked angrily. "I said to leave me alone.

Just then a policeman came up. "Is there any problem, ma'am?" he asked.

"No problem here, officer," the woman answered. "I'm just trying to get this man to his feet. Will you help me?"

The officer scratched his head. "That's old Jack. He's been a fixture around here for a couple of years. What do you want with him?"

"See that cafeteria over there?" she asked. "I'm going to get him something to eat and get him out of the cold for a while."

"Are you crazy, lady?" the homeless man resisted. "I don't want to go in there!" Then he felt strong hands grab his other arm and lift him up. "Let me go, officer. I didn't do anything."

"This is a good deal for you, Jack" the officer answered. "Don't blow it..."

Finally, and with some difficulty, the woman and the police officer got Jack into the cafeteria and sat him at a table in a remote corner. It was the middle of the morning, so most of the breakfast crowd had already left and the lunch bunch had not yet arrived...

The manager strode across the cafeteria and stood by his table. "What's going on here, officer?" he asked. "What is all this, is this man in trouble?"

"This lady brought this man in here to be fed," the policeman answered.

"Not in here!" the manager replied angrily. "Having a person like that here is bad for business..."

Old Jack smiled a toothless grin. "See, lady. I told you so. Now if you'll let me go. I didn't want to come here in the first place."

The woman turned to the cafeteria manager and smiled..... "Sir, are you familiar with Eddy and Associates, the banking firm down the street?"

"Of course I am," the manager answered impatiently. "They hold their weekly meetings in one of my banquet rooms."

"And do you make a goodly amount of money providing food at these weekly meetings?"

"What business is that of yours?"

I, sir, am Penelope Eddy, president and CEO of the company."

"Oh."

The woman smiled again. "I thought that might make a difference." She glanced at the cop who was busy stifling a giggle. "Would you like to join us in a cup of coffee and a meal, officer?"

"No thanks, ma'am," the officer replied. "I'm on duty."

"Then, perhaps, a cup of coffee to go?"

"Yes, mam. That would be very nice."

The cafeteria manager turned on his heel, "I'll get your coffee for you right away, officer."

The officer watched him walk away. "You certainly put him in his place," he said.

"That was not my intent. Believe it or not, I have a reason for all this."

She sat down at the table across from her amazed dinner guest. She stared at him intently.. "Jack, do you remember me?"

Old Jack searched her face with his old, rheumy eyes. "I think so -- I mean you do look familiar."

"I'm a little older perhaps," she said. "Maybe I've even filled out more than in my younger days when you worked here, and I came through that very door, cold and hungry."

"Ma'am?" the officer said questioningly. He couldn't believe that such a magnificently turned out woman could ever have been hungry.

"I was just out of college," the woman began.. "I had come to the city looking for a job, but I couldn't find anything. Finally I was down to my last few cents and had been kicked out of my apartment. I walked the streets for days. It was February and I was cold and nearly starving. I saw this place and walked in on the off chance that I could get something to eat."

Jack lit up with a smile. "Now I remember," he said.. "I was behind the serving counter. You came up and asked me if you could work for something to eat. I said that it was against company policy."

"I know," the woman continued. "Then you made me the biggest roast beef sandwich that I had ever seen, gave me a cup of coffee, and told me to go over to a corner table and enjoy it. I was afraid that you would get into trouble... Then, when I looked over and saw you put the price of my food in the cash register, I knew then that everything would be all right."

"So you started your own business?" Old Jack said.

"I got a job that very afternoon. I worked my way up. Eventually I started my own business that, with the help of God, prospered." She opened her purse and pulled out a business card.. "When you are finished here, I want you to pay a visit to a Mr. Lyons...He's the personnel director of my company. I'll go talk to him now and I'm certain he'll find something for you to do around the office." She smiled. "I think he might even find the funds to give you a little advance so that you can buy some clothes and get a place to live until you get on your feet.... If you ever need anything, my door is always opened to you."

There were tears in the old man's eyes. "How can I ever thank you?" he said.

"Don't thank me," the woman answered. "To God goes the glory. Thank Jesus..... He led me to you."

Outside the cafeteria, the officer and the woman paused at the entrance before going their separate ways.....

"Thank you for all your help, officer," she said.

"On the contrary, Ms. Eddy," he answered. "Thank you. I saw a miracle today, something that I will never forget. .And thank you for the coffee."

If you have missed knowing me, you have missed nothing.

If you have missed some of my emails, you might have missed a laugh...

But, if you have missed knowing my Lord and Savior, Jesus Christ, you have missed everything in the world.

Have a Wonderful Day. May God bless you always and don't forget that when you "cast your bread upon the waters," you never know how it will be returned to you.

God is so big He can cover the whole world with his Love and so small He can curl up inside your heart.

When God leads you to the edge of the cliff, trust Him fully and let go.

Only 1 of 2 things will happen, either He'll catch you when you fall, or He'll teach you how to fly!

****

Better than a Flu Shot!

Miss Beatrice, The church organist, was in her eighties and had never been married.

She was admired for her sweetness and kindness to all.

One afternoon the pastor came to call on her and she showed him into her quaint sitting room.

She invited him to have a seat while she prepared tea. As he sat facing her old Hammond organ, the young minister noticed a cute glass bowl sitting on top of it.

The bowl was filled with water, and in the water Floated, of all things, a condom!

When she returned with tea and scones, they began to chat. The pastor tried to stifle his curiosity about the bowl of water and its strange floater, but soon it got the better of him and he could no longer resist.

'Miss Beatrice', he said,

'I wonder if you would tell me about this.'

Pointing to the bowl.

'Oh, yes,' she replied, 'isn’t it wonderful?

I was walking through the park a few months ago and I found this little package on the ground.

The directions said to place it on the organ, keep it wet and that it would prevent the spread of disease. Do you know I haven't had the flu all winter?'

****

All the organs of the body were having a meeting, trying to decide who the one in charge was.

"I should be in charge," said the brain, “Because I run all the body's systems, so without me nothing would happen."

"I should be in charge," said the blood, “because I circulate oxygen all over so without me you'd all waste away."

"I should be in charge," said the stomach, “because I process food and give all of you energy."

"I should be in charge," said the legs, “because I carry the body wherever it needs to go."

"I should be in charge," said the eyes, “Because I allow the body to see where it goes."

"I should be in charge," said the rectum, “Because I'm responsible for waste removal."

All the other body parts laughed at the rectum and insulted him, so in a huff, he shut down tight.

Within a few days, the brain had a terrible headache, the stomach was bloated, the legs got wobbly, the eyes got watery, and the blood was toxic. They all decided that the rectum should be the boss. The Moral of the story? The ass hole is usually the one in charge!

****

Your Duck is Dead--

A woman brought a very limp duck into a veterinary surgeon. As she laid her pet on the able, the vet pulled out his stethoscope and listened to the bird's chest.

After a moment or two, the vet shook his head and sadly said, "I'm sorry, your duck, cuddles, has passed away."

The distressed woman wailed, "Are you sure?" "Yes, I am sure. Your duck is dead," replied the vet..

"How can you be so sure?" she protested. "I mean you haven't done any testing on him or anything. He might just be in a coma or something."

The vet rolled his eyes, turned around and left the room. He returned a few minutes later with a black Labrador retriever.

As the duck's owner looked on in amazement, the dog stood on his hind legs, put his front paws on the examination table and sniffed the duck from top to bottom. He then looked up at the vet with sad eyes and shook his head.

The vet patted the dog on the head and took it out of the room. A few minutes later he returned with a cat. The cat jumped on the table and also delicately sniffed the bird from head to foot. The cat sat back on its haunches, shook its head, meowed softly and strolled out of the room.

The vet looked at the woman and said, "I'm sorry, but as I said, this is most definitely, 100% certifiably, a dead duck."

The vet turned to his computer terminal, hit a few keys and produced a bill, which he handed to the woman..

The duck's owner, still in shock, took the bill. "$ 500!"She cried, "$500 just to tell me my duck is dead!"

The vet shrugged, "I'm sorry. If you had just taken my word for it, the bill would have been $ 100, but with the Lab Report

****

These are genuine clips from British Council flat tenants complaining to the Council about problems with their apartments!!

1. My bush is really overgrown round the front and my back passage has fungus growing in it.

2. He's got this huge tool that vibrates the whole house and I just can't take it anymore.

3. Its the dog's mess that I find hard to swallow.

4. I want to complain about the farmer across the road; every morning at 6am his cock wakes me up and it's now getting too much for me.

5. I am a woman living in a downstairs flat and would you please do something about the noise made by the man on top of me every night.

6. And their 18-year-old son is continually banging his balls against my fence.

7. Please send a man with the right tool to finish the job and satisfy my wife.

8. My lavatory seat is cracked, where do I stand?

9. I am writing on behalf of my sink, which is coming away from the wall.

10. Will you please send someone to mend the garden path? My wife tripped and fell on it yesterday and now she is pregnant.

11. I request permission to remove my drawers in the kitchen.

12. 50% of the walls are damp, 50% have crumbling plaster and 50% are plain filthy.

13. I am still having problems with smoke in my new drawers.

14. The toilet is blocked and we cannot bath the children until it is cleared.

15. Will you please send a man to look at my water, it is a funny color & not fit to drink.

16. I want some repairs done to my cooker as it has backfired and burnt my knob off.

17. The man next door has a large erection in the back garden, which is unsightly and dangerous.

18. Our kitchen floor is damp. We have two children and would like a third so please send someone round to do something about it.

19. I wish to complain that my father hurt his ankle very badly when he put his foot in the hole in his back passage.

20. I wish to report that tiles are missing from the outside toilet roof. I think it was bad wind the other night that blew them off.

****

PERFECT EXAMPLE OF CONFIDENCE: -

A trainee in a big multinational company dialed CEO by mistake & said, "Hey, send a hot coffee in accounts Department in 2 min"

CEO shouted: Do you know with whom u are talking?

Trainee: NO

CEO: I am CEO of the Company.

Trainee in the same tone: Do you know with whom you are talking?

CEO: No

Trainee said: Thank God!!!!!!!!!!!!!!!!!!!& disconnected the phone

****

A guy walks into a bar with his pet monkey. He orders a drink and while he's drinking, the monkey starts jumping all over the place. The monkey grabs some olives off the bar and eats them, then grabs some sliced limes and eats them, then jumps up on the pool table, grabs the cue ball, sticks it in his mouth and swallows it whole

The bartender screams at the guy, "Did you see what your monkey just did?"

The guy says, "No, what?"

"He just ate the cue ball off my pool table - whole!" says the bartender.

"Yeah, that doesn't surprise me," replies the patron. "He eats everything in sight, the little twerp. I'll pay for the cue ball and stuff."

He finishes his drink, pays his bill, and leaves.

Two weeks later he's in the bar again, and he has his monkey with him. He orders a drink and the monkey starts running around the bar again. While the man is drinking, the monkey finds a cherry on the bar. He grabs it, sticks it up his butt, pulls it out, and eats it.

The bartender is disgusted. "Did you see what your monkey did now?"

"Now what" asks the patron?

"Well, he stuck a cherry up his butt, then pulled it out and ate it!" says the barkeeper.

"Yeah, that doesn't surprise me," replies the patron. "He still eats everything in sight, but ever since he ate that damn cue ball he measures everything first!"

****

Men's Pearls of Wisdom:

1. When I was born, I was given a choice - A big member or a good memory. I don't remember, what I chose.

2. Your birth certificate is an apology letter from the condom factory.

3. A wife is a sex object. Every time you ask for sex, she objects.

4. Impotence: Nature's way of saying 'No hard feelings....'

5. There are only two four letter words that are offensive to men - 'don't' and 'stop', unless they are used together.

6. Panties: Not the best thing on earth, but next to the best thing on earth.

7. There are three stages of sex in a man's life: Tri Weekly, Try Weekly, and Try Weakly.

8. Virginity can be cured.

9. Virginity is not dignity, its lack of opportunity.

10. Having sex is like playing bridge. If you don't have a good partner, you'd better have a good hand.

11. I tried phone sex once, but the holes in the dialer were too small.

12. Marriage is the only war where you get to sleep with the enemy.

13. Q: What's an Australian kiss?

A: The same thing as a French kiss, only down under.

14. A couple just married were happy with the whole thing. He was happy with the Hole and he was happy with the Thing......

15.. Q: What are the three biggest tragedies in a man's life?

A: Life sucks, job sucks, and the wife doesn't..

16. Q: Why do men find it difficult to make eye contact?

A: Breasts don't have eyes.

17. Despite the old saying, ' Don't take your troubles to bed', many men

Still sleep with their wives!!

****

Lawyers should never ask grandma a question if they aren't prepared for the answer.

In a trial, a small-town prosecuting attorney called his first witness, an elderly grandmother to the stand.

He approached her and asked, "Mrs. Jones, do you know me?"

She responded, "Why, yes, I do know you, Mr. Williams. I've known you since you were a young boy, and frankly, you're a big disappointment to me. You lie, cheat on your wife, manipulate people and talk about them behind their backs. You think you're a big shot when you haven't the brains to realize you never will amount to anything more than a two-bit paper pusher. Yes, I know you."

The lawyer was stunned! Not knowing what else to do, he pointed across the room and asked, "Mrs. Jones, do you know the defense attorney?"

She again replied, "Why, yes, I do. I've known Mr. Bradley since he was a youngster. He's lazy, bigoted, and has a drinking problem. He can't build a normal relationship with anyone and his law practice is one of the worst in the state. Not to mention he cheats on his wife with three different women. One of them is your wife. Yes I know him."

The defense attorney almost died.

The judge asked both lawyers to approach the bench and in a quiet voice said: "If either of you idiots asks her if she knows me, I'll send you to the electric chair."

These are from a book called 'Disorder in the American Courts' and are things people actually said in court, word for word, taken down and now published by court reporters that had the torment of staying calm while these exchanges were actually taking place.

ATTORNEY: This myasthenia gravis, does it affect your memory at all?

WITNESS: Yes.

ATTORNEY: And in what ways does it affect your memory?

WITNESS: I forget.

ATTORNEY: You forget? Can you give us an example of something you forgot?

ATTORNEY: Now doctor, isn't it true that when a person dies in his sleep, he doesn't know about it until the next morning?

WITNESS: Did you actually pass the bar exam?

ATTORNEY: The youngest son, the twenty-year-old, how old is he?

WITNESS: He's twenty, much like your IQ.

ATTORNEY: Were you present when your picture was taken?

WITNESS: Are you shitting me?

ATTORNEY: So the date of conception (of the baby) was August 8th?

WITNESS: Yes.

ATTORNEY: And what were you doing at that time?

WITNESS: getting laid

ATTORNEY: She had three children, right?

WITNESS: Yes.

ATTORNEY: How many were boys?

WITNESS: None.

ATTORNEY: Were there any girls?

W ITNESS: Your Honor, I think I need a different attorney. Can I get a new attorney?

ATTORNEY: How was your first marriage terminated?

WITNESS: By death.

ATTORNEY: And by whose death was it terminated?

WITNESS: Take a guess.

ATTORNEY: Can you describe the individual?

WITNESS: He was about medium height and had a beard.

ATTORNEY: Was this a male or a female?

WITNESS: Unless the Circus was in town I'm going with male.

ATTORNEY: Is your appearance here this morning pursuant to a deposition notice which I sent to your attorney?

WITNESS: No, this is how I dress when I go to work.

ATTORNEY: Doctor, how many of your autopsies have you performed on dead people?

WITNESS: All of them. The live ones put up too much of A fight.

ATTORNEY: ALL your responses MUST be oral, OK? What school did you go to?

WITNESS: Oral.

ATTORNEY: Do you recall the time that you examined the body?

WITNESS: The autopsy started around 8:30 p.m.

ATTORNEY: And Mr. Denton was dead at the time?

WITNESS: If not, he was by the time I finished.

ATTORNEY: Are you qualified to give a urine sample?

WITNESS: Are you qualified to ask that question?

And the best for last:

ATTORNEY: Doctor, before you performed the autopsy, did you check for a pulse?

WITNESS: No.

ATTORNEY: Did you check for blood pressure?

WITNESS: No.

ATTORNEY: Did you check for breathing?

WITNESS: No.

ATTORNEY: So, then it is possible that the patient was alive when you began the autopsy?

WITNESS: No.

ATTORNEY: How can you be so sure, Doctor?

WITNESS: Because his brain was sitting on my desk in a jar.

ATTORNEY: I see, but could the patient have still been alive, nevertheless?

WITNESS: Yes, it is possible that he could have been alive and practicing law.

****

Liberally yours...literally yours..

English from Around the World

In a Bangkok temple:

IT IS FORBIDDEN TO ENTER A WOMAN, EVEN A FOREIGNER, IF DRESSED AS A MAN.

Cocktail lounge, Norway:

LADIES ARE REQUESTED NOT TO HAVE CHILDREN IN THE BAR.

Doctor's office, Rome:

SPECIALIST IN WOMEN AND OTHER DISEASES.

Dry cleaners, Bangkok:

DROP YOUR TROUSERS HERE FOR THE BEST RESULTS.

in a Nairobi restaurant:

CUSTOMERS WHO FIND OUR WAITRESSES RUDE OUGHT TO SEE THE MANAGER.

On the main road to Mombassa, leaving Nairobi:

TAKE NOTICE: WHEN THIS SIGN IS UNDER WATER, THIS ROAD IS IMPASSABLE.

On a poster at Kencom:

ARE YOU AN ADULT THAT CANNOT READ? IF SO WE CAN HELP.

In a City restaurant:

OPEN SEVEN DAYS A WEEK AND WEEKENDS.

In a cemetery:

PERSONS ARE PROHIBITED FROM PICKING FLOWERS FROM ANY BUT THEIR OWN GRAVES.

Tokyo hotel's rules and regulations:

GUESTS ARE REQUESTED NOT TO SMOKE OR DO OTHER DISGUSTING BEHAVIOURS IN BED.

On the menu of a Swiss restaurant:

OUR WINES LEAVE YOU NOTHING TO HOPE FOR.

In a Tokyo bar:

SPECIAL COCKTAILS FOR THE LADIES WITH NUTS.

Hotel, Yugoslavia:

THE FLATTENING OF UNDERWEAR WITH PLEASURE IS THE JOB OF THE CHAMBERMAID.

Hotel, Japan:

YOU ARE INVITED TO TAKE ADVANTAGE OF THE CHAMBERMAID.

In the lobby of a Moscow hotel across from a Russian Orthodox monastery:

YOU ARE WELCOME TO VISIT THE CEMETERY WHERE FAMOUS RUSSIAN AND SOVIET COMPOSERS, ARTISTS AND WRITERS ARE BURIED DAILY EXCEPT THURSDAY.

A sign posted in Germany's Black Forest:

IT IS STRICTLY FORBIDDEN ON OUR BLACK FOREST CAMPING SITE THAT PEOPLE OF DIFFERENT SEX, FOR INSTANCE, MEN AND WOMEN, LIVE TOGETHER IN ONE TENT UNLESS THEY ARE MARRIED WITH EACH OTHER FOR THIS PURPOSE.

Hotel, Zurich:

BECAUSE OF THE IMPROPRIETY OF ENTERTAINING GUESTS OF THE OPPOSITE SEX IN THE BEDROOM, IT IS SUGGESTED THAT THE LOBBY BE USED FOR THIS PURPOSE.

Advertisement for donkey rides, Thailand:

WOULD YOU LIKE TO RIDE ON YOUR OWN ASS?

Airline ticket office, Copenhagen:

WE TAKE YOUR BAGS AND SEND THEM IN ALL DIRECTIONS.

A laundry in Rome:

LADIES, LEAVE YOUR CLOTHES HERE AND SPEND THE AFTERNOON HAVING A GOOD TIME.

****

If Columbus had been married, he might never have discovered America, because he would have had to answer all the following questions:

Where are you going? With whom? Why? How are you going? To discover what? Why only you?

What do I do when you are not here? Can I come with you? When will you be back? Will you be home for dinner? What will you bring for me? You deliberately made this plan without me, didn't you? You seem to be making a lot of these programs lately...Answer me why? I want to go to my mother's house. I want you to drop me there. I don't want to come back ever! What do you mean, OK? Why aren't you stopping me? I don't understand what this whole 'discovery' thing is about.

You always do things like this. Last time also you did the same thing! Nowadays you always seem to do this kind of stuff. I still don't understand what else is left to be discovered!

*****

NO Speak English

A Russian woman married a Canadian gentleman and they lived happily ever after in Toronto. The poor lady was not very proficient in English, but did manage to communicate with her husband. The real problem arose whenever she had to shop for groceries.

One day, she went to the butcher and wanted to buy chicken legs. She didn't know how to put forward her request, so, in desperation, clucked like a chicken and lifted up her skirt to show her thighs. Her butcher got the message and gave her the chicken legs.

Next day she needed to get chicken breasts, again she didn't know how to say it, so she clucked like a chicken and unbuttoned her blouse to show the butcher her breasts. The butcher understood again and gave her some chicken breasts.

On the 3rd day, the poor lady needed to buy sausages. Unable to find a way to communicate this, she brought her husband to the store....

What were you thinking?

Her husband speaks English!

****

The Story of Adam & Eve's Pets

Adam and Eve said, 'Lord, when we were in the garden, you walked with us every day. Now we do not see you anymore. We are lonesome here, and it is difficult for us to remember how much you love us.'

And God said, 'I will create a companion for you that will be with you and who will be a reflection of my love for you, so that you will love me even when you cannot see me. Regardless of how selfish or childish or unlovable you may be, this new companion will accept you as you are and will love you as I do, in spite of yourselves..'

And God created a new animal to be a companion for Adam and Eve.

And it was a good animal.

And God was pleased.

And the new animal was pleased to be with Adam and Eve and he wagged his tail

And Adam said, 'Lord, I have already named all the animals in the Kingdom and I cannot think of a name for this new animal.'

And God said, 'I have created this new animal to be a reflection of my love for you, his name will be a reflection of my own name, and you will call him DOG.'

And Dog lived with Adam and Eve and was a companion to them and loved them.

And they were comforted

And God was pleased.

And Dog was content and wagged his tail.

After a while, it came to pass that an angel came to the Lord and said, 'Lord, Adam and Eve have become filled with pride. They strut and preen like peacocks and they believe they are worthy of adoration. Dog has indeed taught them that they are loved, but perhaps too well.'

And God said, 'I will create for them a companion who will be with them and who will see them as they are. The companion will remind them of their limitations, so they will know that they are not always worthy of adoration.'

And God created CAT to be a companion to Adam and Eve.

And Cat would not obey them. And when Adam and Eve gazed into Cat's eyes, they were reminded that they were not the supreme beings.

And Adam and Eve learned humility.

And they were greatly improved.

And God was pleased. . .

And Dog was happy....

And Cat didn't give a shit one way or the other....

*****

Sometimes it DOES take a Rocket Scientist!! (True story)

Scientists at Rolls Royce built a gun specifically to launch dead chickens at the windshields of airliners and military jets all traveling at maximum velocity. The idea is to simulate the frequent incidents of collisions with airborne fowl to test the strength of the windshields.

American engineers heard about the gun and were eager to test it on the windshields of their new high speed trains. Arrangements were made, and a gun was sent to the American engineers.

When the gun was fired, the engineers stood shocked as the chicken hurled out of the barrel, crashed into the shatterproof shield, smashed it to smithereens, blasted through the control console, snapped the engineer's back-rest in two and embedded itself in the back wall of the cabin like an arrow shot from a bow..

The horrified Yanks sent Rolls Royce the disastrous results of the experiment, along with the designs of the windshield and begged the British scientists for suggestions.

(You're going to love this......)

Rolls Royce responded with a one-line memo:

"Defrost the chicken!

****

A duck hunter was out enjoying a nice morning on the marsh when he decided to take a leak......

He walked over to a tree & propped up his gun.

Just then a gust of wind blew, the gun fell over & discharged......

Shooting him in the genitals.

Several hours later lying in a hospital bed, his Doctor met him.

Dr. "Well sir, I have some good news & some bad news, the good news is that you are going to be okay. The damage was local to your groin. There was very little internal damage & we were able to remove all of the buckshot.

Hunter: "What is the bad news?"

Dr. "The bad news is that there was some pretty extensive buckshot damage done to your penis. I am going to have to refer you to my sister. "

Hunter: "Well, I guess that isn't too bad! Is your sister a plastic surgeon? "

Dr. "Not exactly. She is a flute player in the Syracuse Symphony. She is going to teach you where to put your fingers so that you don't piss into your eyes! "

****

The dentist pulls out a numbing needle to give the man a shot. 'No way! No needles. I hate needles' the patient said.

The dentist starts to hook up the nitrous oxide and the man objects.

'I can't do the gas thing. The thought of having that is suffocating me!'

The dentist then asks the patient if he has any objection to taking a pill.

'No objection,' the patient says. 'I'm fine with pills.'

The dentist then returns and says, 'Here's a Viagra tablet. .'The patient says, 'Wow! I didn't know Viagra worked as a pain killer!'

'It doesn't' said the dentist, 'but it's going to give you something to hold onto when I pull your tooth!

****

VERY

INTERESTING STUFF In the 1400's a law was set forth in England that a man was allowed to beat his wife with a stick no thicker than his thumb. Hence we have 'the rule of thumb'

Many years ago in Scotland, a new game was invented. It was ruled 'Gentlemen Only...Ladies Forbidden'....and thus, the word GOLF entered into the English language.

The first couple to be shown in bed together on prime time TV was Fred and Wilma

Flintstone.

Every day more money is printed for Monopoly than the U.S. Treasury.

Men can read smaller print than women can; women can hear better.

Coca-Cola was originally green.

It is impossible to lick your elbow. At least 75% of people who read this will try to lick their elbow

---

The State with the highest percentage of people who walk to work: Alaska

---

The percentage of Africa that is wilderness: 28% (now get this...)

The percentage of North America that is wilderness: 38%

The cost of raising a medium-size dog to the age of eleven: $ 16,400

The average number of people airborne over the U.S. in any given hour: 61,000

Intelligent people have more zinc and copper in their hair..

The first novel ever written on a typewriter, Tom Sawyer.

Each king in a deck of playing cards represents a great king from history:

Spades - King David

Hearts - Charlemagne

Clubs -Alexander, the Great

Diamonds - Julius Caesar

111,111,111 x

111,111,111 = 12,345,678,987, 654,321

If a statue in the park of a person on a horse has both front legs in the air, the person died in battle. If the horse has one front leg in the air, the person died because of wounds received in battle. If the horse has all four legs on the ground, the person died of natural causes

----

Only two people signed the Declaration of Independence on July 4, John Hancock and Charles Thomson. Most of the rest signed on August 2, but the last signature wasn't added until 5 years later.

Q. Half of all Americans live within 50 miles of what?

A. Their birthplace

Q. Most boat owners name their boats. What is the most popular boat name requested?

A. Obsession

Q. If you were to spell out numbers, how far would you have to go until you would find the letter 'A'?

A. One thousand

Q. What do bulletproof vests, fire escapes, windshield wipers and laser printers have in common?

A. All were invented by women.

Q. Which day are there more collect calls than any other day of the year?

A. Father's Day

In Shakespeare's time, mattresses were secured on bed frames by ropes. When you pulled on the ropes, the mattress tightened, making the bed firmer to sleep on. Hence the phrase...'Goodnight. Sleep tight'

It was the accepted practice in Babylon 4,000 years ago that for a month after the wedding, the bride's father would supply his son-in-law with all the mead he could drink. Mead is a honey beer and because their calendar was lunar based, this period was called the honey month, which we know today as the honeymoon.

In English pubs, ale is ordered by pints and quarts... So in old England. When customers got unruly, the bartender would yell at them 'Mind your pints and quarts, and settle down.'

It's where we get the phrase 'mind your P's and Q's' years ago in England. Pub frequenters had a whistle baked into the rim, or handle, of their ceramic cups. When they needed a refill, they used the whistle to get some service. 'Wet your whistle' is the phrase inspired by this practice.

Don't skip this just because it looks weird. Believe it or not, you can read it.

I cdnuolt blveiee taht I cluod aulaclty uesdnatnrd waht I was rdanieg. The phaonmneal pweor of the hmuan mnid Aoccdrnig to rscheearch at Cmabrigde Uinervtisy, it deosn't mttaer in waht oredr the ltteers in a wrod are, the olny iprmoatnt tihng is taht the first and last ltteer be in the rghit pclae. The rset can be a taotl mses and you can still raed it wouthit a porbelm. This is bcuseae the huamn mnid deos not raed ervey lteter by istlef, but the wrod as a wlohe. Amzanig huh?

****

Pain of a married man!!!!!

A woman awakes during the night to find that her husband was not in bed.

She goes downstairs to look for him. She finds him sitting at the kitchen table with a cup of coffee in front of him.

He appears to be in deep thought, just staring at the wall. She watches as he wipes a tear from his eye and takes a sip of his coffee.

"What's the matter, dear?" she whispers as she steps into the room. "Why are you down here at this time of night?"

The husband looks up from his coffee, "Do you remember 20 years ago when we were dating, and you were only 18?" he asks solemnly. "Yes I do" she replies.

The husband pauses; the words were not coming easily. "Do you remember when your father caught us in the garden?"

"Yes, I remember" said the wife, lowering herself into a chair beside him.

The husband continued. "Do you remember when he showed the shotgun in my face and said, 'Either you marry my daughter, or I'll send you to jail for 20 years?"

"I remember that too" she replied softly.

He wiped another tear from his cheek and said, "I would have been released today!"

I never quite figured out why the sexual urge of men and women differ so much. And I never have figured out the whole Venus and Mars thing. I have never figured out why men think with their head and women with their heart.

FOR EXAMPLE:

One evening last week, my girlfriend and I were getting into bed.

Well, the passion starts to heat up, and she eventually says, 'I don't feel like it,

I just want you to hold me.'

I said, 'WHAT??!! What was that?!'

So she says the words that every boyfriend on the planet dreads to hear...

'You're just not in touch with my emotional needs as a woman enough for me to satisfy your physical needs as a man.'

She responded to my puzzled look by saying,

'Can't you just love me for who I am and not what I do for you in the bedroom?'

Realizing that nothing was going to happen that night, I went to sleep.

The very next day I opted to take the day off of work to spend time with her.

We went out to a nice lunch and then went shopping at a big, big unnamed department store.

I walked around with her while she tried on several different very expensive outfits.

She couldn't decide which one to take, so I told her we'd just buy them all.

She wanted new shoes to compliment her new clothes, so I said, 'Let's get a pair for each outfit.'

We went on to the jewelry department where she picked out a pair of diamond earrings.

Let me tell you... she was so excited. She must have thought I was one wave short of a shipwreck.

I started to think she was testing me because she asked for a tennis bracelet when she doesn't even know how to play tennis.

I think I threw her for a loop when I said, 'That's fine, honey.'

She was almost nearing sexual satisfaction from all of the excitement.

Smiling with excited anticipation, she finally said, 'I think this is all dear, let's go to the cashier.'

I could hardly contain myself when I blurted out, 'No honey, I don't feel like it.'

Her face just went completely blank as her jaw dropped with a baffled, 'WHAT?'

I then said, 'Honey! I just want you to HOLD this stuff for a while.

You're just not in touch with my financial needs as a man enough for me to satisfy your shopping needs as a woman.'

And just when she had this look like she was going to kill me, I added,

'Why can't you just love me for who I am and not for the things I buy you?'

Apparently I'm not having sex tonight either....but at least she knows I'm smarter than her.

THINGS YOU CAN ONLY SAY AT CHRISTMAS

1: I prefer breasts to legs.

2: Tying the legs together keeps the inside moist.

3: Smother the butter all over the breasts.

4: If I don't undo my trousers, I'll burst!

5: I've never seen a better spread!

6: I fancy a little dark meat for a change.

7: Are you ready for seconds yet?

8: It's a little dry, do you still want to eat it?

9: Just wait your turn, you'll get some!

10: Don't play with your meat!

11: Stuff it up between the legs as far as it will go.

12: Do you think you'll be able to handle all these people at once?

13: I didn't expect everyone to come at the same time!

14: You still have a little bit on your chin.

15: How long will it take after you put it in?

16: You'll know it's ready when it pops up.

17: Just pull the end and wait for the bang.

18: That's the biggest bird I've ever had!

19: I'm so full, I've been gobbling nuts all morning.

20: Wow, I didn't think I could handle all that and still want more.

Old Age, I decided, is a gift

I am now, probably for the first time in my life, the person I have always wanted to be. Oh, not my body! I sometime despair over my body, the wrinkles, the baggy eyes, and the sagging butt. And often I am taken aback by that old person that lives in my mirror (who looks like my mother!), but I don't agonize over those things for long..

I would never trade my amazing friends, my wonderful life, my loving family for less gray hair or a flatter belly. As I've aged, I've become kinder to myself, and less critical of myself. I've become my own friend.

I don't chide myself for eating that extra cookie, or for not making my bed, or for buying that silly cement gecko that I didn't need, but looks so Avant grade on my patio. I am entitled to a treat, to be messy, to be extravagant.

I have seen too many dear friends leave this world too soon; before they understood the great freedom that comes with aging.

Whose business is it if I choose to read or play on the computer until 4 AM and sleep until noon?

I will dance with myself to those wonderful tunes of the 60&70's, and if I, at the same time, wish to weep over a lost love... I will.

I will walk the beach in a swim suit that is stretched over a bulging body, and will dive into the waves with abandon if I choose to, despite the pitying glances from the jet set.

They, too, will get old.

I know I am sometimes forgetful. But there again, some of life is just as well forgotten. And I eventually remember the important things.

Sure, over the years my heart has been broken. How can your heart not break when you lose a loved one, or when a child suffers, or even when somebody's beloved pet gets hit by a car? But broken hearts are what give us strength and understanding and compassion. A heart never broken is pristine and sterile and will never know the joy of being imperfect.

I am so blessed to have lived long enough to have my hair turning gray, and to have my youthful laughs be forever etched into deep grooves on my face. So many have never laughed, and so many have died before their hair could turn silver

As you get older, it is easier to be positive. You care less about what other people think. I don't question myself anymore. I've even earned the right to be wrong.

So, to answer your question, I like being old. It has set me free. I like the person I have become. I am not going to live forever, but while I am still here, I will not waste time lamenting what could have been, or worrying about what will be. And I shall eat dessert every single day. (If I feel like it)

MAY YOUR FRIENDSHIP NEVER COME APART ESPECIALLY WHEN IT'S STRAIGHT FROM THE HEART! MAY YOU ALWAYS HAVE A RAINBOW OF SMILES ON YOUR FACE AND IN YOUR HEART FOREVER AND EVER!

RE: THE TOMATO STORY

You Will Know What Is Better When It Comes To Earning Money

Tomato Story

A Jobless man applied for the position of 'office boy' at Microsoft.

The HR manager interviewed him then watched him cleaning the floor as a test.

'You are employed' he said. Give me your e-mail address and I'll send you the application to fill in, as well as date when you may start.

The man replied 'But I don't have a computer, neither an email'.

'I'm sorry', said the HR manager. If you don't have an email, that means you do not exist. And who doesn't exist, cannot have the job.'

The man left with no hope at all. He didn't know what to do, with only $10 in his pocket. He then decided to go to the supermarket and buy a 10Kg tomato crate.

He then sold the tomatoes in a door to door round. In less than two hours, he succeeded to double his capital. He repeated the operation three times, and returned home with $60.

The man realized that he can survive by this way, and started to go every day earlier, and return late. Thus, his money doubled or tripled every day.

Shortly, he bought a cart, then a truck, and then he had his own fleet of delivery vehicles.

5 years later, the man is one of the biggest food retailers in the US

He started to plan his family's future, and decided to have a life insurance.

He called an insurance broker, and chose a protection plan.

When the conversation was concluded the broker asked him his email.

The man replied, 'I don't have an email.'

The broker answered curiously, 'You don't have an email, and yet have succeeded to build an empire. Can you imagine what you could have been if you had an e mail?!!' The man thought for a while and replied, 'Yes, I'd be an office boy at Microsoft!'

Moral of the story

Moral 1

Internet is not the solution to your life.

Moral 2

If you don't have Internet, but work hard, you can be a millionaire.

Moral 3

If you received this message by email, you are closer to being an office boy/girl, than a millionaire. ....

A man called home his wife and said, "Honey I have been asked to go fishing up in Canada with my boss and several of his friends. We'll be gone for a week. This is good opportunity for me to get that promotion I've been wanting so could you please pack enough clothes for a week and set out my rod and fishing box? We're leaving

From the office and I will swing by the house to pick my things up.

Oh! Please pack my new blue silk pajamas."

The wife thinks this sounds a bit fishy but being the good wife she, did exactly what her husband asked.

The following weekend he came home a little tired but otherwise looking good. The wife welcomed him home and asked if he caught many fish? He said, "Yes! Lots of Salmon, some bluegill, and a few swordfish. But why didn't you pack my new blue silk pajamas like I asked you to do?

You'll love the answer....

The wife replied, "I did. They're in your fishing box!"

LAW OF THE JUNGLE

Two guys were hiking through the jungle when they spotted a tiger that looked both hungry and fast. One of the guys reached into his pack and pulled out a pair of Nike.

His friend looked at him "Do you really think those shoes are going to make you run faster than that tiger?" I don't have to run faster than that tiger, his friend replied. "I just have to run faster than you"\

WELCOME TO The corporate world!!

A father put his three year old daughter to bed, told her a story and listened to her prayers which she ended by saying

"God bless Mommy, God bless daddy, and God bless grandma and good-bye grandpa."

The father asked, "Why did you say good-bye grandpa?"

The little girl said, "I don't know daddy, it just seemed like the thing to do."

The next day grandpa died.

The father thought it was a strange coincidence.

A few months later the father put the girl to bed and listened to her prayers, which went like this:

"God bless Mommy, God Bless daddy and good-bye grandma."

The next day the grandmother died.

Oh my god, thought the father, this kid is in contact with the other side

Several weeks later when the girl was going to bed the dad heard her say,

"God bless Mommy and good-bye daddy."

He practically went into shock.

He couldn't sleep all night and got up at the crack of dawn to go to his office .He was nervous as a cat all day, had lunch sent in and watched the clock.

He figured if he could get by until midnight he would be okay. He felt safe in the office, so instead of going home at the end of the day he stayed there, looking at his watch and jumping at every sound.

Finally midnight arrived, he breathed a sigh of relief and went home.

When he got home his wife said

"I've never seen you work so late, what's the matter?"

He said "I don't want to talk about it, I've just spent the worst day of my life."

She said "You think you had a bad day, you'll never believe what happened

HERE.

He asked "What"??????

She said "This morning our neighbor James suddenly died."

****

Irony of life but true! :)

Men:

1. All men are extremely busy.

2. Although they are so busy, they still have time for women.

3. Although they have time for women, they don't really care for them.

4. Although they don't really care for them, they always have one around.

5. Although they always have one around them, they always try their luck

With others.

6. Although they try their luck with others, they get really pissed off if

The woman leaves them.

7. Although the woman leaves them, they still don't learn from their

Mistakes, and still try their

Luck with others.

Women:

1. the most important thing for a woman is financial security.

2. Although this is so important, they still go out and buy expensive Clothes and stuff.

3. Although they always buy expensive clothes, they never have something to Wear.

4. Although they never have something to wear, they always dress beautifully.

5. Although they always dress beautifully, their clothes are always just "An old rag".

6. Although their clothes are always "just an old rag", they still expect you to compliment them.

7. Although they expect you to compliment them, when you do, they don't believe you.

****

Honesty is the best policy....

Jack decided to go skiing with his buddy, Bob. So they loaded up Jack's minivan and headed north. After driving for a few hours, they got caught in a terrible blizzard. So they pulled into a nearby farm and asked the attractive lady who answered the door if they could spend the night.

"I realize its terrible weather out there and I have this huge house all to myself, but I'm recently widowed," she explained. "I'm afraid the neighbors will talk if I let you stay in my house."

"Don't worry," Jack said. "We'll be happy to sleep in the barn. And if the weather breaks, we'll be gone at first light."

The lady agreed, and the two men found their way to the barn and settled in for the night. Come morning, the weather had cleared, and they got on their way.

They enjoyed a great weekend of skiing.

But about nine months later, Jack got an unexpected letter from an attorney. It took him a few minutes to figure it out, but he finally determined that it was from the attorney of that attractive widow he had met on the ski weekend.

He dropped in on his friend Bob and asked, "Bob, do you remember that good-looking widow from the farm we stayed at on our ski holiday up north AB out 9 months ago?"

"Yes, I do." said Bob

"Did you, ER, happen to get up in the middle of the night, go up to the house and pay her a visit?"

"Well, um, yes!," Bob said, a little embarrassed about being found out, "I have to admit that I did."

"And did you happen to give her my name instead of telling her your name?"

Bob's face turned beet red and he said, "Yeah, look, I'm sorry, buddy. I'm afraid I did. Why do you ask?"

"She just died and left me everything."

****

1. If you won't dress like the Victoria's Secret girls, don't expect us to act like soap opera guys.

****

1. If you think you're fat, you probably are. Don't ask us.

****

1. If something we said can be interpreted two ways and one of the ways makes you sad or angry, we meant the other one

****

1. You can either ask us to do something or tell us how you want it done. Not both.

If you already know best how to do it, just do it yourself.

****

1. Whenever possible, Please say whatever you have to say during commercials.

****

1. Christopher Columbus did NOT need directions and neither do we.

****

1. ALL men see in only 16 colors, like Windows default settings.

Peach, for example, is a fruit, not a color. Pumpkin is also a fruit. We have no idea what mauve is.

****

1. If we ask what is wrong and you say "nothing," We will act like nothing's wrong.

We know you are lying, but it is just not worth the hassle.

****

1. If you ask a question you don't want an answer to, expect an answer you don't want to hear.

****

1. When we have to go somewhere, absolutely anything you wear is fine. Really.

****

1. Don't ask us what we're thinking about unless you are prepared to discuss such topics as baseball, the shotgun formation, or golf.

****

1. You have enough clothes.

****

1. You have too many shoes.

****

1. I am in shape. Round IS a shape!

****

1. Thank you for reading this.

Yes, I know, I have to sleep on the couch tonight;

****

The last one is classic!

A grade one teacher collected well known proverbs. She gave each child in her class the first half of a proverb and asked them to come up with the remainder of the proverb. It's hard to believe these were actually done by grader one kids ("6 "year-olds),

Don't bite the hand that looks dirty.

If you lie down with dogs, you'll stink in the morning.

No news is impossible.

You can't teach an old dog new maths.

Love all, trust me.

The pen is mightier than the pigs.

Where there's smoke there's pollution.

A penny saved is not much.

Two's company, three's the Musketeers.

Laugh and the whole world laughs with you, cry and you have to blow your nose.

There are none so blind as Stevie Wonder.

When the blind leadeth the blind get out of the way.

And the favorite: Better late than pregnant!

****

A tour bus driver is driving with a bus load of seniors down a highway when he is tapped on his shoulder by a little old lady.

She offers him a handful of peanuts, which he gratefully munches up.

After about 15 minutes, she taps him on his shoulder, again and she hands him another handful of peanuts.

She repeats this gesture about five more times.

When she is about to hand him another batch again he asks the little old lady,

"Why don`t you eat the peanuts yourself?”

"We can't chew them because we've no teeth", she replied.

The puzzled driver asks,

"Why do you buy them then?"

The old lady replied,

"We just love the chocolate around them."

Men's Logic

A man and his wife were in a court for their divorce case. The Problem was who should get custody of the child.

The wife screamed and jumped up and said: "Your Honor. I brought the child into the world with all the pain and labor.

The child should be in my custody."

The judge turned to the husband and said: "What do you have to Say in your defense?"

The man sat for a while contemplating. ..Then slowly rose. "Your Honor... If I put a dollar in a Pepsi Vending Machine and a Pepsi comes out...

Whose Pepsi is it...? The machines or mine?"

****

Today is World Happy Husband Day.

Let us keep 2 minutes silence and read some quotes of great personalities.

First quote

After marriage, husband and wife become two sides of a coin, they just can't face each other, but still they stay together.

– Al Gore

By all means marry. If you get a good wife, you'll be happy. If you get a bad one, you'll become a philosopher.

– Socrates

Wife inspires us to great things and prevent us from achieving them.

– Mike Tyson

I had some words with my wife, and she had some paragraphs with me.

– Bill Clinton

There's a way of transferring funds that is even faster than electronic banking. It's called marriage.

– Michael Jordan

A good wife always forgives her husband when she's wrong.

– Barack Obama

When you are in love, wonders happen.

But once you get married, you wonder, what happened.

- Steve Jobs

And the best one is…

Marriage is a beautiful forest where Brave Lions are killed by Beautiful Deer.

- Brad Pitt

World Happy Husband Day!!

Laughter Therapy

While getting married, most of the guys say to girl's parents,

"I will keep your daughter happy for the rest of her life".

Have you ever heard a girl saying something like this to the boy's parents like "I will keep your son happy for the rest of his life"????

Nooo.... because women don't tell lies!

****

Husband and wife are setting up a new computer at home. The system asked to generate a new password.

The husband cheekily keyed in “My Penis ".

Wife burst out laughing when the system responded with - “Error. Not long enough.

****

I DON'T KNOW HOW THEY WROTE THIS WITH A STRAIGHT FACE...

This was a real memo sent out by IBM to its employees in all seriousness. It went to all field engineers about a computer peripheral problem. The author of this memo was quite genuine.

The engineers rolled on the floor! Especially note the last couple of sentences.

"If a mouse fails to operate or should it perform erratically, it may need a ball replacement. Mouse balls are now available as FRU (Field Replacement Units). Because of the delicate nature of this procedure, replacement of mouse balls should only be attempted by properly trained personnel. Before proceeding, determine the type of mouse balls by examining the underside of the mouse. Domestic balls will be larger and harder than foreign balls.

Ball removal procedures differ depending upon the manufacturer of the mouse. Foreign balls can be replaced using the pop off method. Domestic balls are replaced by using the twist off method. Mouse balls are not usually static sensitive. However, excessive handling can result in sudden discharge.

Upon completion of ball replacement, the mouse may be used immediately. It is recommended that each person have a pair of spare balls for maintaining optimum customer satisfaction.

Any customer missing his balls should contact the local personnel in charge of removing and replacing these necessary items. Please keep in mind that a customer without properly working balls is an unhappy customer."

****

Ernesto, the caretaker

At dawn, the telephone rings..."Hello, Senor Smith? This is Ernesto ... the caretaker at your country house."

"Ah yes, Ernesto. What can I do for you? Is there a problem?"

Uh...I'm just calling to advise you, Senor that your parrot died."

"My parrot? Dead? The one that won the International speaking competition?"

"Si, Senor...that's the one."

"Damn! That's a pity! I spent a small fortune on that bird. What did he die from?"

"From eating rotten meat, Senor."

"Rotten meat? Who the hell fed the parrot rotten meat?"

"Nobody, Senor, he ate the meat of your dead horse!"

"Dead horse? What dead horse?!"

"The thoroughbred that won the Breeders Cup, Senor Smith. He died from a heart attack pulling the big water cart."

"Are you insane? What water cart?"

"The one we used to put out the fire, Senor!"

"Good Lord! What fire are you talking about, man?"

"The one at your house, Senor! A candle fell and the curtains caught on fire "

"What the...!! There's electricity at the house!! What the hell was the candle for?"

"For the funeral, Senor."

"WHAT BLOODY FUNERAL?!"

"Your wife's, Senor... She showed up one night out of the blue and I thought she was a thief... So I hit her with your new Tiger Woods Nike driver."

A long pause of complete silence...

"Ernesto, if you broke that driver, you're in deep shit!!!!!!"

****

Washington Post limerick contest

The Washington Post runs a weekly limerick contest in its Style section called the Style Invitational.

The requirements this week were to use the two names Lewinsky (The Intern) and Kaczynski (the UN bomber) in the same limerick.

The following are the winning entries; remember, they were printed in the newspaper!

Third place:

There once was a gal named Lewinsky

Who played on a flute like Stravinsky

T' was Hail to the Chief

On this flute made of beef

That stole the front page from Kaczynski.

Second place:

Said Clinton to young Ms. Lewinsky,

We don't want to leave clues like Kaczynski

Since you made such a mess,

Use the hem of your dress

And please wipe that stuff off your chinsky.

And the winning entry:

Lewinsky and Clinton have shown

What Kaczynski must surely have known?

That an intern is better

Than a bomb in a letter

When deciding how best to be blown.

PS: Gives a new meaning to the saying "there's a sucker born every minute”

****

Subject: The Patch

Two priests were in a Vatican bathroom using the urinals.

One of them looked at the other one's penis & noticed a nicoderm patch on it.

He turned to the other priest & said, "I believe you're supposed to put that patch on your arm or shoulder, not on your penis."

The other one replied, "Actually, it's working just fine. I’m down to 2 butts a day!"

****

Musharraf calls Bush on 11th September:

Musharraf: Mr. President, I would like to express my condolences to you. It is a real tragedy. So many people, such great buildings...

I would like to ensure that we had nothing in connection with that........

Bush: What buildings? What people??

Musharraf: Oh, and what time is it in America now?

Bush: It's eight in the morning.

Musharraf: Oops...Will call back in an hour!

****

Vajpayee and Bush are sitting in a bar. A guy walks in and asks the barman, "Isn't that Bush and Vajpayee?"

The barman says "Yep, that's them." So the guy walks over and says,

"Hello, what are you guys doing?"

Bush says, "We're planning world war 3"

The guy says, "Really? What's going to happen?"

And Vajpayee says, "Well, we're going to kill 14 million Pakistanis and one bicycle repairman."

And the guy exclaimed, "a bicycle repairman?!!!"

Vajpayee turns to Bush and says, "See, I told you no-one would worry about the 14 million Pakistanis!"

****

Rahul went hunting one day in Ontario and bagged three ducks. He put them in the bed of his pickup truck and was about to drive home when he was confronted by an ornery game warden who didn't like Rahul and friends.

The game warden ordered Rahul to show his hunting license, and Rahul pulled out a valid Ontario hunting license. The game warden looked at the license, then reached over and picked up one of the ducks, sniffed its butt, and said, "This duck ain't from Ontario. This is a Quebec duck. You got a Quebec huntin' license, boy?"

The Rahul reached into his wallet and produced a Quebec hunting license. The game warden looked at it, then reached over and grabbed the second duck, sniffed its butt, and said "This ain't no Quebec duck. This duck's from Manitoba. You got a Manitoba license?" Rahul reached into his wallet and produced a Manitoba hunting license.

The warden then reached over and picked up the third duck, sniffed its butt, and said, "This ain't no Manitoba duck. This here duck's from Nova Scotia. You got a Nova Scotia huntin' license?" Again Rahul reached into his wallet and brought out a Nova Scotia hunting license.

The game warden was extremely frustrated at this point, and he yelled At Rahul "Just where the hell are you from?"

Rahul smiled turned around, bent over, dropped his pants showing his butts and said, "You tell me, you're the expert."

****

Several men are in the locker room of a golf club. A cell phone on a bench rings and a man engages the hands-free speaker function and begins to talk.

Everyone else in the room stops to listen.

MAN: "Hello"

WOMAN: "Honey, it's me. Are you at the club?"

MAN: "Yes"

WOMAN: "I am at the mall now and found this beautiful leather coat. It's only $1,000. Is it OK if I buy it?"

MAN: "Sure, go ahead if you like it that much."

WOMAN: "I also stopped by the Mercedes dealership and saw the new 2005 models. I saw one I really liked."

MAN: "How much?"

WOMAN: "$80,000"

MAN: "OK, but for that price I want it with all the options."

WOMAN: "Great! Oh, and one more thing....the house we wanted last year is back on the market. They're asking $950,000."

MAN: "Well, then go ahead and give them an offer, but just offer $900,000."

WOMAN: "OK. I'll see you later! I love you!"

MAN: "Bye, I love you, too."

The man hangs up. The other men in the locker room are looking at him in astonishment.

Then he asks: "Anyone know who this phone belongs to??!!"

****

Foreign Signs in English

People in other countries sometimes go out of their way to communicate with their English-speaking tourists.

Here is a list of signs seen around the world.

At a Budapest zoo:

PLEASE DO NOT FEED THE ANIMALS. IF YOU HAVE ANY SUITABLE FOOD, GIVE IT TO THE GUARD ON DUTY.

Doctor's office, Rome:

SPECIALIST IN WOMEN AND OTHER DISEASES.

Information booklet about using a hotel air conditioner, Japan:

COOLES AND HEATES: IF YOU WANT CONDITION OF WARM AIR IN YOUR ROOM, PLEASE CONTROL YOURSELF

On an Athi River highway:

TAKE NOTICE: WHEN THIS SIGN IS UNDER WATER, THIS ROAD IS IMPASSABLE.

On a poster at Kencom:

ARE YOU AN ADULT THAT CANNOT READ? IF SO, WE CAN HELP.

In a City restaurant:

OPEN SEVEN DAYS A WEEK, AND WEEKENDS TOO.

In a cemetery

PERSONS ARE PROHIBITED FROM PICKING FLOWERS FROM ANY BUT THEIR OWN GRAVES.

On the menu of a Swiss restaurant:

OUR WINES LEAVE YOU NOTHING TO HOPE FOR.

Hotel elevator, Paris:

PLEASE LEAVE YOUR VALUES AT THE FRONT DESK.

In an East African newspaper:

A NEW SWIMMING POOL IS RAPIDLY TAKING SHAPE SINCE THE CONTRACTORS HAVE THROWN IN THE BULK OF THEIR WORKERS.

EVER WONDER....

Why do we have to click on “Start" in order to shutdown windows?

Why the sun lightens our hair, but darkens our skin?

Why is "abbreviated" such a long word?

Why is lemon juice made with artificial flavor, and dishwashing liquid made with real lemons?

Why the man who invests all your money is called a broker?

Why is the time of day with the slowest traffic called rush hour?

Why isn't there mouse-flavored cat food?

Why do they sterilize the needle for lethal injections?

You know that indestructible black box that is used on airplanes? Why don't they make the whole plane out of that stuff?!

Why don't sheep shrink when it rains?

Why are they called apartments when they are all stuck together?

If con is the opposite of pro, is Congress the opposite of progress?

If flying is so safe, why do they call the airport the terminal?

****

During an inspection, the GOC asked a young Lt

"Son, what are your duties in the unit?"

Lt: "Sir, I am the sexual adviser to the CO"

There was a stunned silence all around.

GOC in shock, asked, “How?”

The Lt said, “Sir, the CO has told me, When I need your fucking advice, I will ask for it"

****

Kulula is a low-cost South-African airline that doesn't take itself too seriously. Kulula airline attendants make an effort to make the in-flight announcements a bit more entertaining☟:

**

On another flight with a very "senior" flight attendant crew, the pilot said, “Ladies and gentlemen, we've reached cruising altitude and will be turning down the cabin lights. This is for your comfort and to enhance the appearance of your flight attendants."

**

On landing, the stewardess said "Please be sure to take all of your belongings.. If you're going to leave anything, please make sure it's something we'd like to have."

**

"There may be 50 ways to leave your lover, but there are only 4 ways out of this airplane."

**

"Thank you for flying Kulula. We hope you enjoyed giving us the business as much as we enjoyed taking you for a ride."

**

"As you exit the plane, make sure to gather all of your belongings. Anything left behind will be distributed evenly among the flight attendants. Please do not leave spouses..."

Overheard on a Kulula flight into Cape Town, after an extremely hard landing, the Flight Attendant said," Ladies and Gentlemen, welcome to The Mother City. Please remain in your seats with your seat belts fastened while the Captain taxis what's left of our airplane to the gate!"

**

The airline had a policy which required the first officer to stand at the door while the passengers exited, smile, and give them a "Thanks for flying our airline". He said that, in light of his bad landing, he had a hard time looking the passengers in the eye, thinking that someone would have a smart comment. Finally everyone had gotten off except for a little old lady walking with a cane. She said, "Sir, do you mind if I ask you a question?"

"Why, no Ma'am," said the pilot. "What is it?"

The little old lady said, "Did we land, or were we shot down?"

**

Heard on a Kulula flight:

"Ladies and gentlemen, if you wish to smoke, the smoking section on this airplane is on the wing. If you can light'em, you can smoke'em."

****

THERE ARE 3 KINDS OF MEN...

1. THE EUROPEANS

They have 1 wife and 1 girlfriend but they love their wife the most.

2 THE AMERICANS

They have 1 wife and 1 girlfriend but they love their girlfriend the most...

3. THE INDIANS

They have 1 wife and 4 girlfriends but they love their mother the most...

And the special one. --

THE ARABS

They have 4 wives and 4 girlfriends. But they love their camel the most!!

Vallaah Habibi!!.....😝😝

****

Did you know this???

For Railway Crossings in India there are MALE LEVEL CROSSINGS and FEMALE LEVEL CROSSINGS...!!!😨

Can you guess how they are distinguished..??

Read this...!!!

An inquiry was being held for an accident at a railway crossing in Punjab.

A Station Master was asked by the Inquiry Commission:

"How many railway crossings are there in your area?"

Station Master replies:

"There are totally 11 railway crossings; 4 are unmanned and 7 are manned crossings. Of the 7 manned crossings, 4 are male & 3 are female your Honor."

After a brief silence, the Inquiry Commission asked?

"What do you mean by 'male' and 'female' crossings? Please explain?"

To which the Station Master replies:

"Where the barrier pole goes up, we call it male and where the gates spread open we call it female"...!!!

Some officials nearly fainted!!!

We love the Indian Railways.

****

Retirement Dinner

A priest was being honored at his retirement Dinner after 25 years in the parish. A leading local Politician and member of the congregation was chosen to make the presentation and give a little speech at the Dinner.

However, he was delayed, so the priest, Decided to say his own few words while they Waited:

'I got my first impression of the parish from the first confession I heard here. I thought I had been assigned to a terrible place. The very first person who entered my confessional told me he had stolen a television

Set and, when questioned by the police, was able to lie his way out of it. He had stolen money from his parents, Embezzled from his employer, had an affair with his Boss's wife, taken Illegal drugs, and beat up his sister. I was appalled.

But as the days went on, I learned that my people were not all like that and I had, indeed, come to a fine parish full of good and loving people.'...

Just as the priest finished his talk, the politician arrived full of apologies at being late.

He immediately began to make the presentation and gave his talk:

'I'll never forget the first day our parish priest arrived,' said the politician. 'In fact, I had the honor of being the first person to go to him for confession.'

Moral: Never, Never, Never Be Late!

****

A little boy got on the bus, sat next to a man reading a book, and noticed he had his collar on backwards. The little boy asked why he wore his collar backwards.

The man, who was a Priest, said:

'I am a Father.'

The little boy replied:

'My Daddy doesn't wear his collar like that.'

The priest looked up from his book and answered:

'I am the Father of many.'

The boy said: 'My Dad has 4 boys, 4 girls and two grandchildren and he doesn't wear his collar that way!'

The Priest, getting impatient, said: 'I am the Father of hundreds' and went back to reading his book.

The little boy sat quietly thinking for a while, then leaned over and said:

'Maybe you should wear a condom and your pants backwards instead of your collar.'

****

The rain was pouring down heavily in M.G. Road, Bengaluru. And standing in front of a big puddle outside a pub, was an old Parsi Uncle, drenched, and holding a stick, with a piece of string dangling in the water.

Arun, a passer-by stopped and asked, "What are you doing, uncle?"

"Fishing" replied the old man.

Feeling sorry for the old man, Arun said, "Come out of the rain and have a drink with me, uncle."

In the warmth of the pub, as they sip their whiskies, Arun cannot resist asking, "So how many fish have you caught today?"

"You're the eighth" says the old Parsi .

****

Yorkshire farmer

A farmer in Yorkshire sees a bloke drinking from his stream & shouts: "Ey up cocker, tha dunt wanna be drinkin watta frum theer, its full o hoss piss an cow shite."

The bloke says: "Sir, I am from Pakistan. Can you be speaking clearer, and slower please?"

The farmer replies: "If you use two hands you won't spill any"

****

Only the Irish have Jokes like These

Into a Belfast pub comes Paddy Murphy, looking like he'd just been run over by a train.

His arm is in a sling, his nose is broken, his face is cut and bruised and he's walking with a limp

"What happened to you?" asks Sean, the bartender.

"Jamie O'Conner and me had a fight," says Paddy.

"That little shit, O'Conner," says Sean,

"He couldn't do that to you, he must have had something in his hand."

"That he did," says Paddy, "a shovel is what he had, and a terrible lickin' he gave me with it."

"Well," says Sean, "you should have defended yourself; didn't you have something in your hand?"

That I did," said Paddy.

"Mrs. O'Conner's breast, and a thing of beauty it was, but useless in a fight."

****

An Irishman who had a little too much to drink, is driving home from the city one night and, of course, his car is weaving violently all over the road.

A cop pulls him over. “So," says the cop to the driver, where have ya been?"

"Why, I've been to the pub of course," slurs the drunk.

"Well," says the cop, "it looks like you've had quite a few to drink this evening."

"I did all right," the drunk says with a smile. “Did you know," says the cop, standing straight and folding his arms across his chest, "that a few inter sections back, your wife fell out of your car?"

"Oh, thank heavens," sighs the drunk. “For a minute there, I thought I'd gone deaf."

****

Brenda O'Malley is home making dinner, as usual, when Tim Finnegan arrives at her door.

"Brenda, may I come in?" he asks. “I’ve something' to tell ya".

"Of course you can come in, you're always welcome, Tim.

But where's my husband?"

"That's what I'm here to be telling ya, Brenda."

There was an accident down at the Guinness brewery..."

"Oh, God no!" cries Brenda. "Please don't tell me."

"I must, Brenda. Your husband Shamus is dead and gone. I'm sorry.

Finally, she looked up at Tim.

"How did it happen, Tim?"

"It was terrible, Brenda. He fell into a vat of Guinness Stout and drowned."

"Oh my Dear Jesus! But you must tell me truth, Tim.

Did he at least go quickly?"

"Well, Brenda... no. In fact, he got out three times to pee."

****

Mary Clancy goes up to Father O'Grady after his Sunday morning service, and she's in tears.

He says, "So what's bothering you, Mary my dear?"

She says, "Oh, Father, I've got terrible news.

My husband passed away last night."

The priest says, "Oh, Mary, that's terrible.

Tell me, Mary, did he have any last requests?"

She says, "That he did, Father."

The priest says, "What did he ask, Mary?"

She says, He said, 'Please Mary, put down that damn gun...'

****

AND THE BEST FOR LAST

A drunk staggers into a Catholic Church, enters a confessional booth, sits down, but says nothing. The Priest coughs a few times to get his attention but the drunk continues to sit there.

Finally, the Priest pounds three times on the wall.

The drunk mumbles, "ain't no use knockin, there's no paper on this side either!"

****

At the end of the tax year, the Tax Office sent an inspector to Audit the books of a synagogue.

While he was checking the books he turned to the Rabbi and said: "I notice you buy a lot of candles. What do you do with the candle drippings?"

"Good question," noted the Rabbi. "We save them up and send them back to the candle makers, and every now and then they send us a free box of candles."

"Oh," replied the auditor, somewhat disappointed that his unusual Question had a practical answer. But on he went, in his obnoxious way "What about all these biscuit purchases? What do you do with the crumbs?

"Ah, yes," replied the Rabbi, realizing that the inspector was trying to trap him with an answerable question

"We collect them and send them back to the manufacturers, and every now and then they send a free box of holy biscuits."

"I see," replied the auditor, thinking hard about how he could fluster the know-it-all Rabbi.

"Well, Rabbi," he went on, "what do you do with all the leftover foreskins from the circumcisions you perform?"

"Here, too, we do not waste," answered the Rabbi. "What we do is save up all the foreskins and send them to the Tax Office, and about once a year they send us a complete prick".

****

The foreign minister of a small African state had opportunity to visit Russia for the very first time. There he was warmly welcomed by his Russian counterpart, who wined and dined him and generally offered him the best hospitality that Russia could offer.

On his last day, the Russian foreign minister took the African foreign minister into a room with a table on which lay a revolver. "My comrade, since you are about to leave, I must introduce you to a custom we have here in Russia, something called Russian Roulette. It is a true test of manhood and worth, and how it works is that you must take the revolver, spin the cylinders, hold the revolver to your head and then pull the trigger. Only one of the six chambers is loaded."

The African leader, being of proud warrior stock and a courageous man, took the revolver, spun the cylinder, snapped it shut, pointed it at his head and sighed with relief when all he heard was 'click', but no shot.

Well impressed with his bravery, he and the Russian drank vodka until the African leader had to be carried aboard his plane.

Six months later the Russian foreign minister visits the African foreign minister's country. The African, remembering keenly the Russian roulette he had to play previously, took the Russian into a room on the last day of his visit. In the room were six beautiful, naked young women.

"To prove your courage and manhood, see before you six of the most beautiful women from each of our tribes. This is something we call 'African Roulette'. You may pick any one of them and they will give you a blowjob."

The Russian, not too averse to this idea at all, asks the African, "But where is the risk? To be called roulette there must be some form of risk involved."

The African smiles broadly. "One of the six is a cannibal!"

****

THIS IS AN OLD ONE, BUT WORTH READING AGAIN.

The priest in a small Irish village loved the rooster and ten hens

He kept them in the hen house behind the church.

One Sunday morning, before mass, he went to feed the birds and discovered that the cock was missing.

He knew about cock fights in the village, so he questioned his parishioners in church.

During mass, he asked the congregation, 'Has anybody got a cock?'

All the men stood up.

'No, no,' he said, 'that wasn't what I meant. Has anybody seen a cock?'

All the women stood up.

'No, no,' he said, 'that wasn't what I meant.

Has anybody seen a cock that doesn't belong to them?'

Half the women stood up.

'No, no,' he said, 'that wasn't what I meant.

Has anybody seen *MY cock?*

Sixteen altar boys, two priest sand a goat stood up,

The priest fainted.

****

COFFEE TABLE

Four Catholic men and a Catholic woman were having coffee.

The first Catholic man tells his friends, "My son is a priest, when he walks into a room, and everyone calls him 'Father'."

The second Catholic man chirps, "My son is a Bishop. When he walks into a room people call him 'Your Grace'."

The third Catholic gent says, "My son is a Cardinal. When he enters a room everyone says 'Your Eminence'."

The fourth Catholic man then says, "My son is the Pope. When he walks into a room people call him 'Your Holiness'."

Since the lone Catholic woman was sipping her coffee in silence, the four men give her a subtle, "Well....?"She proudly replies, "I have a daughter, slim, tall, 38D breast, 24" waist and 34" hips. When she walks into a room, people say, "Oh My God."

****

VATICAN HUMOR

After getting all of Pope Benedict's luggage loaded into the limo, (and he doesn't travel light), the driver notices the Pope is still standing on the curb.

'Excuse me, Your Holiness,' says the driver, 'Would you please take your seat so we can leave?'

'Well, to tell you the truth,' says the Pope, 'they never let me drive at the Vatican when I was a cardinal, and I'd really like to drive today.'

'I'm sorry, Your Holiness, but I cannot let you do that. I'd lose my job! What if something should happen?' protests the driver, wishing he'd never gone to work that morning.

'Who's going to tell?' says the Pope with a smile.

Reluctantly, the driver gets in the back as the Pope climbs in behind the wheel. The driver quickly regrets his decision when, after exiting the airport, the Pontiff floors it, accelerating the limo to 205 kmph.. (Remember, the Pope is German...)

'Please slow down, Your Holiness!' pleads the worried driver, but the Pope keeps the pedal to the metal until they hear sirens.

'Oh, dear God, I'm going to lose my license -- and my job!' moans the driver.

The Pope pulls over and rolls down the window as the cop approaches, but the cop takes one look at him, goes back to his motorcycle, and gets on the radio.

'I need to talk to the Chief,' he says to the dispatcher.

The Chief gets on the radio and the cop tells him that he's stopped a limo going 205 kmph.

'So bust him,' says the Chief.

'I don't think we want to do that, he's really important,' said the cop.

The Chief exclaimed,' All the more reason!'

'No, I mean really important,' said the cop with a bit of persistence.

The Chief then asked, 'who do you have there, the mayor?'

Cop: 'Bigger.'

Chief: ' A senator?'

Cop: 'Bigger.'

Chief: 'The Prime Minister?'

Cop: 'Bigger.'

'Well,' said the Chief, 'who is it?'

Cop: 'I think it's God!'

The Chief is even more puzzled and curious, 'What makes you think it's God?'

Cop: 'His chauffeur is the Pope!'

****

One day the priest was called away for an emergency. Not wanting to leave the confessional unattended, He called Paddy D'Costa (his new assistant) and asked him to cover for him.

Paddy told him he wouldn't know what to say, but the priest told him to stay with him for a little while and learn what to do.

Paddy joined the priest and then followed him into the confessional. A few minutes later a woman came in and said "Father, forgive me for I have sinned"

Priest: "What did you do?"

Woman: "I committed adultery"

Priest: "How many times?"

Woman: "Three times"

Priest: "Say Two Hail Mary's, put $ 5.00 in the charity box, and sin no more"

A few minutes later a man entered the confessional.

He said "Father, forgive me for I have sinned"

Priest: "What did you do?"

Man: "I committed adultery"

Priest: "How many times?"

Man: "Three times"

Priest: "Say two Hail Mary's, put $ 5.00 in the charity box, and sin no more,

Paddy, a quick learner, told the priest that he understood the job and the priest could leave. Santa D'costa was now alone. A few minutes later another woman entered and said "Father, forgive me for I have sinned"

Paddy: "What did you do?"

Woman: "I committed adultery"

Paddy: "How many times?"

Woman: "Once"

Paddy: "Go do it two more times, we have a special offer this week, three times for $ 5.00"

****

Each Friday night after work, Abdul would fire up his outdoor grill and cook a tandoori chicken and some meat kebabs. But, all of his neighbors were strict Catholics ... and since it was Lent, they were forbidden from eating chicken and meat on a Friday.

The delicious aroma from the grilled meats was causing such a problem for the Catholic faithful that they finally talked to their Priest. The Priest came to visit Abdul and suggested that he become a Catholic. After several classes and much study, Abdu attended Mass... And as the priest sprinkled holy water over him, he said, you were born a Muslim, and raised a Muslim, but now, you are a Catholic."

Abdu's neighbors were greatly relieved, until Friday night arrived. The wonderful aroma of tandoori chicken and meat kebabs filled the neighborhood. The Priest was called immediately by the neighbors and, as he rushed into Abdu's backyard, clutching a rosary and prepared to scold him, he stopped and watched in amazement.

There stood Abdu, holding a small bottle of holy water which he carefully sprinkled over the grilling meats and chanted: "Oye, you were born a chicken, and you were born a lamb, you were raised a chicken and you were raised a lamb but now you are a potato and tomato"

****

A man sees a woman getting chased by a dog in Chandni Chowk area of New Delhi .

When the dog is about to bite the woman, the man intervenes and kicks the dog.

A Times of India reporter was seeing all this.

He said "That was great.

I'll definitely publish this in our newspaper.

Tomorrow the headline will be 'LOCAL HERO SAVES LADY FROM A DOG'."

The man replied "Thank you, but I'm not from here. I am from US".

Reporter said "OK. Then the headline will be US CITIZEN SAVES WOMAN FROM A DOG ".

Man: Actually, I live in US but I'm not a US citizen.

I'm a Pakistani national by origin".

Next day, the headline in the local newspaper......

Pakistani Terrorist ATTACKS A LOCAL DOG.

****

A big earthquake with the strength of 8.1 on the Richter scale has hit Pakistan.

Two million Pakistanis have died and over a million are injured.

The country is totally ruined and the government doesn't know where to start with providing help to rebuild.

The rest of the world is in shock.

.. The USA is sending troops to help.

.. Saudi Arabia is sending oil.

.. Latin American countries are sending supplies.

.. New Zealand is sending sheep, cattle and food crops.

.. The Asian continents are sending labor to assist in rebuilding infrastructure.

.. Australia is sending medical teams and supplies.

.. Britain, not to be outdone, is sending two million replacement Pakistanis.

****

Singh and an American are seated next to each other on a flight from

Los Angeles to New York. The American asks if he would like to play a fun-game.

Rahul, tired, just wants to take a nap, so he politely declines and rolls over to the window to catch a few winks.

The American persists and explains that the game is easy and a lot of fun.

He says, "I ask you a question, and if you don't know the answer, you pay me $5, and vice versa."

Again, Singh declines and tries to get some sleep.

The American, now worked up, says, "Okay, if you don't know the answer, you pay me $5, and if I don't know the answer, I'll pay you $500."

This gets Rahul's attention and, figuring there will be no end to this torment, agrees to the game.

The American asks the first question, "What's the distance from the earth to the moon?"

Singh doesn't say a word, reaches into his wallet, pulls out a $5 bill and hands it to the American.

"Okay," says the American, "Your turn."

So Singh asks, "What goes up a hill with three legs and comes down with four legs?"

The American thinks about it. No answer.

Puzzled, he takes out his laptop computer and searches all his references. No answer!

He taps into the air-phone with his modem and searches the Internet and the Library of Congress. No answer.

Frustrated, he sends e-mails to all his friends and co-workers. Checks the input. All to no avail!

Finally, a long time later, he wakes Singh and hands him $500.

Singh thanks him and turns back to get his sleep.

The American, more than a little miffed, stirs the

Singh and asks, "Well, what's the answer?"

Without a word, Singh reaches into his purse, hands the American $5,and goes back to sleep!

****

Mrs. Donovan was walking down O'Connell Street in Dublin when she met Father Flaherty.

The Father said, 'Top o' the mornin' to ye! Aren't ye Mrs Donovan, and didn't I marry ye and yer hoosband 2 years ago?'

She replied, 'Aye, that ye did, Fadder.'

The Father asked, 'And be there any wee little ones yet?'

She replied, 'No, not yet, Fadder.'

The Father said, 'Well, now, I'm goin' to Rome next week, 'I'll light a candle for ye and yer hoosband.'She replied,

'Oh, thank ye Fadder. 'They then parted ways.

Some years later, they met again.

The Father asked, 'Well now, Mrs. Donovan, how are ye these days?'

She replied, 'Oh, very well, Fadder!'

The Father asked, and tell me, have ye been blessed with any wee ones yet?'

She replied, 'Oh yes, Fadder! T'ree sets o'twins and 4 singles, 10 in all!'

The Father said, 'That's wonderful! How is your husband doing?

She replied, 'E's gone to Rome to blow out yer fookin' candle.'

****

A woman starts dating a doctor. Before too long, she becomes pregnant and they don't know what to do. About nine months later, just about the time she is going to give birth, a priest goes into the hospital for a prostate gland infection.

The doctor says to the woman, "I know what we'll do. After I've operated on the priest, I'll give the baby to him and tell him it was a miracle."

"Do you think it will work?" she asks the doctor.

"It's worth a try," he says.

So the doctor delivers the baby and then operates on the priest. After the operation he goes in to the priest and says, "Father, you're not going to believe this."

"What?" says the priest? "What happened?"

"You gave birth to a child."

"But that's impossible!"

"I just did the operation," insists the doctor. "It's a miracle! Here's your baby."

About fifteen years go by, and the priest realizes that he must tell his son the truth.

One day he sits the boy down and says, "Son, I have something to tell you. I'm not your father."

The son says, "What do you mean, you're not my father?"

The priest replies, "I'm your mother. The archbishop is your father."

****

Bill Gates organized an enormous session to recruit a new Chairman for Microsoft Europe. 5000 candidates assembled in a large room. One candidate is Santa Singh an Indian (Punjabi) guy.

Bill Gates thanked all the candidates for coming and asking those who do not know JAVA program to leave.2000 people leave the room. Santa says to himself, 'I do not know JAVA but I have nothing to lose if I stay. I'll give it a try'

Bill Gates asked the candidates who never had experience of managing more than 100 people to leave. 2000 people leave the room. Santa says to himself ' I never managed anybody by myself but I have nothing to lose if I stay. What can happen to me?' So he stays.

Then Bill Gates asked candidates who do not have management diplomas to leave. 500 people leave the room. Santa says to himself, 'I left school at 15 but what have I got to lose?' So he stays in the room.

Lastly, Bill Gates asked the candidates who do not speak Serbo - Croat to leave. 498 people leave the room. Santa says to himself, ' I do not speak one word of Serbo - Croat but what do I have to lose?' So he stays and finds himself with one other candidate. Everyone else has gone.

Bill Gates joined them and said 'Apparently you are the only two candidates who speak Serbo - Croat, so I'd now like to hear you have a conversation together in that language.' Calmly, Santa turns to the other candidate and says 'Hor Phaphe ki haal chaal?.' The other candidate answers ' O Vadiya veere, tu Sunna'

****

A cow from Alberta

The only cow in a small town in USA stopped giving milk. The people did some research and found that they could buy a cow from BC Canada for 1,000 dollars, or one from Alberta Canada for 800 dollars. Being poor, they bought the cow from Alberta.

The cow was wonderful. It produced lots of milk all the time, and the people were amazed and very happy.

They decided to acquire a bull to mate with the cow and produce more cows like it. Then they would never have to worry about the milk supply again.

They bought a bull and put it in the pasture with their beloved cow.

However, whenever the bull came close to the cow, the cow would move away. No matter what approach the bull tried, the cow would move away from the bull and he could not succeed in his quest.

The people were very upset and decided to ask the rabbi, who was very wise, what to do.

They told the rabbi what was happening; "Whenever the bull approaches our cow, she moves away. If he approaches from the back, she moves forward. When he approaches her from the front, she backs off. An approach from the side and she just walks away to the other side.

The rabbi thought about this for a minute and asked, "Did you buy this cow from Alberta?"

The people were dumbfounded. They had never mentioned where they had gotten the cow. "You are truly a wise rabbi. How did you know we got the cow from Alberta?

"The rabbi answered sadly, "My wife is from Alberta."

****

Leather bound Bible

A young man was getting ready to graduate from college. For many months he had admired a beautiful sports car in a dealer's showroom, and knowing his father could well afford it, he told him that was all he wanted.

As Graduation Day approached, the young man awaited signs that his father had purchased the car.

Finally, on the morning of his graduation, his father called him into his private study.

His father told him how proud he was to have such a fine son, and told him how much he loved him. He handed his son a beautiful wrapped gift box. Curious, but somewhat Disappointed, the young man opened the box and found a lovely, leather-bound Bible, with the young man's name embossed in gold.

Angrily, he raised his voice to his father and said, “With all your money you give me a Bible? And stormed out of the house, leaving the Bible.

Many years passed and the young man was very successful in business. He had a beautiful home and wonderful family, but realized his father was very old, and thought perhaps he should go to him. He had not seen him since that graduation day.

Before he could make arrangements, he received a telegram telling him his father had passed away, and willed all of his possessions to his son. He needed to come home immediately and take care of things.

When he arrived at his father's house, sudden sadness and regret filled his heart. He began to search through his father's important papers and saw the still new Bible, just as he had left it years ago. With tears, he opened the Bible and began to turn the pages.

His father had carefully underlined a verse, Matt 7:11, "And if ye, being evil know how to give good gifts to your children, how much more shall your Heavenly father which is in heaven, given to those who ask Him?" As he read those words, a car key dropped from the back of the Bible. It had a tag with the dealer's name, the same dealer who had the sports car he had desired. On the tag was the date of his graduation, and the words... PAID IN FULL.

****

God is in joking mood

A man was praying to god.

He said, "God?"

God responded, “Yes?"

And the Guy said, “Can I ask a question?"

"Go right ahead", God said.

"God, what is a million years to you?"

God said, "A million years to me is only a second."

The man wondered.

Then he asked, "God, what is a million dollars’ worth to you?"

God said, "A million dollars to me is a penny."

So the man said, “God can I have a penny?"

And God cheerfully said,

"Sure! Just a second."

Singh to his servant: Go and water the plants.

Servant: It's already raining.

Singh: So what take an umbrella and go?

Singh found the answer to the most difficult question ever -

What will come first, Chicken or egg?

O Yaar, whatever U order first, will come first.

A teacher told all students in a class to write an essay on a cricket match. All were busy writing except one Singh.

He wrote "DUE TO RAIN, NO MATCH!"

Postman: - I Have To Come 5 Miles to Deliver U This Packet

Singh: - why did U come so far. Instead U could Have posted it....

Singh & his wife filed an application for Divorce.

Judge asked: How'll U divide your kids, U"VE 3 children?

Singh replied: Ok! We'll apply NEXT YEAR

Singh's wish: when I die, I wanna die like my Grandpa who died peacefully in his sleep not Screaming like all d passengers in d car he was Driving..

A Teacher lecturing on population:

"In India after every 10 secondss a women gives birth to a kid."

Singh ,stands up- "We must find & stop her!. "

A man: "Singh, tell me, why Manmohan Singh goes for a walk in the evening not in the morning?"

Singh: "Arey bhai Manmohan is PM not AM".

Singh visits Chinese friend dying in hospital.

The Chinese friend just says "CHIN YU YAN" and dies.

Singh goes to China to find the meaning of his friend's last Words.

And finds It means "U R STANDNG ON the OXYGEN TUBE!"

Singh was standing in front of the mirror with his eyes closed.

His wife asked what you are doing.

He said-I am seeing how I look while sleeping.

Why did Singh cut the sides of the capsule before taking it?

Guess what...

To avoid side effects!!!

Man: Singh where were U born?

Singh: Punjab.

Man: Which part?

Singh: Oye part part kya kar raha hai, whole body Is born in Punjab Yaar".

Lawyer toSingh: "Gita pe haath rakhkar kaho ke......"

Singh :"Yeh kya, sita pe haath lagaya to court mein Bulaya. Ab fir gita pe haath!!"

ASingh saw a beautiful girl... He went and kissed her....

Girl said- "What R U doing...?"

Singh replied- "B.COM from Khalsa college, Chandigar"

Singh: For the past one week a girl is disturbing me.

I don't know how she got my no, she interrupts whenever I call someone and says "please recharge your card"

****

A person went into the office kitchen one morning and found a Singh"s sister painting the walls. She was wearing a new fur coat and a nice denim jacket. Thinking this was a little strange; he asked her why she was wearing them rather than old clothes or an overall.

She showed him the instructions on the tin, "For Best Results put on Two Coats"

****

Singh was drawing money from ATM,

Rahul behind him in the line said, "Ha! Ha! Haaa! I've seen ur password. Its 4 asterisks (****). "

Singh replies, "Ha! Ha! Haaa! U R wrong, its 1258"

Q:) How do U recognize a Singh in school or College???

A:) They are the ones who erase their notebooks when the teacher erases the blackboard... BOLO tarara!!

Q:) Why did Rahulji sleep with a scale?

A :) Because he wanted to measure how long he has slept........

****

An attractive blonde from Dublin arrived at the casino and bet twenty-thousand dollars on a single roll of the dice.

She said, "I hope you don't mind, but I feel much luckier when I'm completely nude."

With that, she stripped from the neck down, rolled the dice and yelled, "Come on, baby, Mama needs new clothes!"

As the dice came to a stop, she jumped up and down and squealed "YES, YES, I WON, I WON!"

She hugged each of the dealers and then picked up her winnings and her clothes and quickly departed.

The dealers stared at each other dumb founded.

Finally, one of them asked, "What did she roll?"

The other answered, "I don't know - I thought you were watching."

MORAL OF THE STORY:-

Not all Irish are stupid. Not all blondes are dumb. But all men are men.

****

IT IS NOT A STORY BUT A TRUE INCIDENT THAT HAPPENED IN AMERICA.

An Indian man walks into a bank in New York City and asks for the loan officer. He tells the loan officer that he is going to India on business for two weeks and needs to borrow $5,000.

The bank officer tells him that the bank will need some form of security for the loan, so the Indian man hands over the keys to a new Ferrari parked on the street in front of the bank. He produces the title and everything checks out. The loan officer agrees to accept the car as collateral for the loan.

The bank's president and its officers all enjoy a good laugh at the Indian for using a $250,000 Ferrari as collateral against a $5,000 loan. An employee of the bank then drives the Ferrari into the bank's underground garage and parks it there.

Two weeks later, the Indian returns, repays the $5,000 and the interest, which comes to $15.41.The loan officer says, "Sir, we are very happy to have had your business, and this transaction has worked out very nicely, but we are a little puzzled. While you were away, we checked you out and found that you are a multi-millionaire. What puzzles us is, why would you bother to borrow "$5,000".

The Indian replies: "Where else in New York City can I park my car for two weeks for only $15.41 and expect it to be there when I return".

Ah, the mind of the Indian...

This is why India is shining...!!!

An American decided to write a book about famous churches around the world.

So he bought a plane ticket and took a trip to china.

On his first day he was inside a church taking photographs when he

Noticed a golden telephone mounted on the wall with a sign that read

"$10,000 per call".

The American, being intrigued, asked a priest who was strolling by

What the telephone was used for.

The priest replied that it was a direct line to heaven and that for

$10,000 you could talk to God.

The American thanked the priest and went along his way.

Next stop was in Japan. There, at a very large

Cathedral, he saw the same golden telephone with the same sign under it.

He wondered if this was the same kind of telephone he saw in china

And he asked a nearby nun what its purpose was.

She told him that it was a direct line to heaven and that for

$10,000 he could talk to God.

"O.K., thank you," said the American.

He then traveled to Pakistan. Sri Lanka, Russia. Germany and France.

In every church he saw the same golden telephone

With the same "$10,000 per call" sign under it.

The American, upon leaving Vermont decided to travel to up to India

To see if Indians had the same phone.

He arrived in India. And again, in the first church he entered,

There was the same golden telephone, but this time the sign under it read "One Rupee per call."

The American was surprised so he asked the priest about the sign.

"Father, I've traveled all over World and I've seen this same golden

Telephone in many churches. I'm told that it is a direct line to

Heaven, but in the US the price was $10,000 per call.

Why is it so cheap here?"

The priest smiled and answered, "You're in India now, son - it's a

Local call".

****

No God or Know God?

An atheist professor of philosophy speaks to his class on the problem Science has with God, The Almighty.

He asks one of his new students to stand.

Prof: So you believe in God?

Student: Absolutely, sir.

Prof: Is God good?

Student: Sure.

Prof: Is God all-powerful?

Student: Yes.

Prof: My brother died of cancer even though he prayed to God to heal him.

Most of us would attempt to help others who are ill. But God didn't. How is this God good then? Hmm? (Student is silent.)

Prof: You can't answer, can you? Let's start again, young fellow. Is God good?

Student: Yes.

Prof: Is Satan good?

Student: No. Prof: Where does Satan come from?

Student: From...God.. .

Prof: That's right. Tell me son, is there evil in this world?

Student: Yes.

Prof: Evil is everywhere, isn't it? And God did make everything. Correct?

Student: Yes.

Prof: So who created evil?

(Student does not answer.)

Prof: Is there sickness? Immorality? Hatred? Ugliness? All these terrible things exist in the world, don't they?

Student: Yes, sir.

Prof: So, who created them?

(Student has no answer.)

Prof: Science says you have 5 senses you use to identify and observe the world around you. Tell me, son...Have you ever seen God?

Student: No, sir.

Prof: Tell us if you have ever heard your God?

Student: No, sir.

Prof: Have you ever felt your God, tasted your God, smelt your God? Have you ever had any sensory perception of God for that matter?

Student: No, sir. I'm afraid I haven't.

Prof: Yet you still believe in Him?

Student: Yes.

Prof: According to empirical, testable, demonstrable protocol, science says your GOD doesn't exist. What do you say to that, son?

Student: Nothing. I only have my faith.

Prof: Yes. Faith. And that is the problem science has.

Student: Professor, is there such a thing as heat?

Prof: Yes.

Student: And is there such a thing as cold?

Prof: Yes.

Student: No sir. There isn't.

(The lecture theatre becomes very quiet with this turn of events.)

Student: Sir, you can have lots of heat, even more heat, superheat, mega heat, white heat, a little heat or no heat. But we don't have anything called cold. We can hit 458 degrees below zero which is no heat,

But we can't go any further after that. There is no such thing as cold. Cold is only a word we use to describe the absence of heat. We cannot measure cold.

Heat is energy. Cold is not the opposite of heat, sir, just the absence of it.

(There is pin-drop silence in the lecture theatre.)

Student: What about darkness, Professor? Is there such a thing as darkness?

Prof: Yes. What is night if there isn't darkness?

Student: You're wrong again, sir. Darkness is the absence of something. You can have low light, normal light, bright light, flashing light....But if you have no light constantly, you have nothing and it's called darkness, isn't it? In reality, darkness isn't.

If it were you would be able to make darkness darker, wouldn't you?

Prof: So what is the point you are making, young man?

Student: Sir, my point is your philosophical premise is flawed.

Prof: Flawed? Can you explain how?

Student: Sir, you are working on the premise of duality. You argue there is life and then there is death, a good God and a bad God. You are viewing the concept of God as something finite, something we can measure.

Sir, science can't even explain a thought. It uses electricity and magnetism, but has never seen, much less fully understood either one.

To view death as the opposite of life is to be ignorant of the fact that death cannot exist as a substantive thing. Death is not the opposite of life: just the absence of it. Now tell me, Professor. Do you teach your students that they evolved from a monkey?

Prof: If you are referring to the natural evolutionary process, yes, of course, I do.

Student: Have you ever observed evolution with your own eyes, sir?

(The Professor shakes his head with a smile, beginning to realize where the argument is going.)

Student: Since no one has ever observed the process of evolution at work and cannot even prove that this process is an on-going Endeavour, are you not teaching your opinion, sir? Are you not a scientist but a preacher?

(The class is in uproar.)

Student: Is there anyone in the class who has ever seen the Professor's brain?

(The class breaks out into laughter.)

Student: Is there anyone here who has ever heard the Professor's brain, felt it, touched or smelt it? No one appears to have done so. So, according to the established rules of empirical, stable, demonstrable protocol, science says that you have no brain, sir.

With all due respect, sir, how do we then trust your lectures, sir?

(The room is silent. The professor stares at the student, his face unfathomable.)

Prof: I guess you'll have to take them on faith, son.

Student: That is it sir... The link between man & god is FAITH.

That is all that keeps things moving & alive....

****

Most Famous Man

One day in a school in London, a teacher said to a class of 5-year-olds, "I'll give 10 pounds to the child who can tell me who was the most famous man who ever lived."

An Irish boy put his hand up and said, "It was St. Patrick." The teacher said, "Sorry Paddy, that's not correct." Then a Scottish boy put his hand up and said, "It was St. Andrew."

The teacher replied, "I'm sorry, Hamish, that's not right either."

Finally, a Gujju (Gujarati) boy raised his hand and said, "It was Jesus Christ."

The teacher said, "That's absolutely right, Raj, come up here and I'll give you the 10 pounds that I promised."

As the teacher was giving Raj his money, she said," You know Raj, since you're a Patel; I was very surprised you said Jesus Christ." Raj replied, "Yes. In my heart I knew it was Krishna, but you know, Business is Business

****

Here is a funny joke about a south Indian boy on his first day at school in the USA.

It was the first day of school and a new student named Chandrashekhar

Subrahmanyam entered the fourth grade.

The teacher said, "Let's begin by reviewing some American History.

Who said "Give me Liberty, or give me Death"?

She saw a sea of blank faces, except for Chandrashekhar, who had his hand

up: "Patrick Henry, 1775" he said.

"Very good!" Who said "Government of the People, by the People, for the

People, shall not perish from the Earth?"

Again, no response except from Chandrashekhar. "Abraham Lincoln, 1863" said

Chandrashekhar.

The teacher snapped at the class, "Class, you should be ashamed.

Chandrashekhar, who is new to our country, knows more! About its history than you do."

She heard a loud whisper: "F**k the Indians,"

"Who said that?" she demanded.

Chandrashekhar put his hand up. "General Custer, 1862."

At that point, a student in the back said, "I'm gonna puke."

The teacher glares around and asks "All right! Now, who said that?"

Again, Chandrashekhar says, "George Bush to the Japanese Prime Minister, 1991."

Now furious, another student yells, "Oh yeah? S*ck this!"Chandrashekhar jumps out of his chair waving his hand and shouts to the teacher, "Bill Clinton, to Monica Lewinsky, 1997!"

Now with almost mob hysteria someone said "You little shit. If you say anything else, I'll kill you."Chandrashekhar frantically yells at the top of his voice, "Gary Condit to Chandra Levy, 2001."

The teacher fainted. And as the class gathered around the teacher on the floor, someone said, "Oh shit, we're f**ked!"

And Chandrashekhar said quietly, "George Bush, Iraq, 2005."

****

A lady approaches her priest and tells him "Father, I have a problem.

I have two female talking parrots, but they only know how to say one

Thing."

"What do they say?" the priest inquired.

"They only know how to say, 'Hi, we're prostitutes.'Want to have some fun?"

"That's terrible!" the priest exclaimed, "but I have a solution to your problem. Bring your two female parrots over to my house and I will put them with my two male talking parrots that I taught to pray and read the bible. My parrots will teach your parrot's to stop saying that terrible phrase and your female parrots will learn

To pray and worship."

"Thank you!" the woman responded.

The next day the woman brings her female parrots to the priest's house.

His two male parrots are holding the rosary beads and praying in their Cage. The lady puts her two female parrots in with the male parrots and the female parrots say "Hi we're prostitutes, want to have some fun?"

One male parrot looks over at the other male parrot and exclaims, "Put the beads away, brother. Our prayers have been answered!"

****

An Irish Joke :(may have been brewed by an English Catholic!!!)

An Irish daughter had not been home for over 5 years.

Upon her return, her father cussed her; "Where have you been all this time, you ingrate! Why didn't you write us, not even a line to let us know how you were doing? Why didn't you call? You little tramp! Don't you know what you put your Mum through??!!"

The girl, crying, replied, "Sniff, sniff... Dad... I became a prostitute..."

"WHAT!!? Out of here, you shameless harlot! Sinner! You're a disgrace to this family - I don't ever want to see you again!"

"OK, Dad - as you wish. I just came back to give Mom this luxury fur coat, title deeds to a ten bed-roomed mansion, plus a savings account certificate for 2 million. For my little brother, this gold Rolex, and for your Daddy the brand spanking new Mercedes limited edition convertible that's parked outside plus a lifetime membership to the Country Club...(takes a breath)...an invitation for you all to spend New Years' Eve on board my new yacht in the Riviera, and...."

"Now what was it you said you had become?

Girl, crying again, "Sniff, sniff... A prostitute Dad! ... Sniff, sniff"

"Oh! Be Jesus! - You scared me half to death, girl! I thought you said a Protestant. Come here and give your old man a hug

****

Interviewer: what's your Date of birth

Singh: 13th October

Which year?

Singh: Oye ullu ke pathe _ _ _ EVERY YEAR

**

Manager asked to Singh at an interview, Can you spell a word that has more than 100 letters in it?

Singh replied: -P-O-S-T-B-O-X.

**

Teacher to Singh: Write your best friend's name in English.

Singh wrote: ' Beautiful Red Underwear'

Teacher: What?

Singh: His name is Sundar Lal Chaddi

**

After returning back from a foreign trip, Singh asked his wife, do I look like a foreigner?

Wife: No! Why?

Singh: In London a lady asked me Are you a foreigner?

***

One tourist from U.S.A. asked to Singh: Any great man born in this village???

Singhr: no sir, only small Babies!!!

***

Lecturer: write a note on Gandhi Jayanthi

So Singh writes, "Gandhi was a great man, but I don't know who is Jayanthi.

***

Singh was doing experiment with cockroach, first he cut it's one leg and told WALK. WALK. Cockroach walked. Then he cut its second leg and told the same. Cockroach walked. Then cut the third leg and did the same. At last he cut its fourth leg and ordered it walk! But cockroach didn't walk. Suddenly Singh said loudly, "I found it. If we cut cockroach's four legs, it becomes deaf.

****

On a political rally Singh was arrested. Why??? A woman journalist walking with a badge wrote "PRESS" and He did it...

***

When Singh was traveling with his wife in an auto, the driver adjusted mirror. Singh shouted, "You are trying to see my wife? Sit back. I will drive.

***

aSingh went in a hotel. To wash hands he went to the washbasin. There he started washing the basin. Seeing this, the manager asked what was he doing. Singh pointed towards the board “WASH BASIN”

***

Interviewer: just imagine you’re in 3rd floor, it caught fire and how will you escape?

Singh: it's simple. I will stop my imagination!!!

***

You see things; and you say, 'Why?' But I dream things that never were; and I say, "Why not?"

****

Bill Gates- After Death

Well, Bill," said God, "I'm really confused on this one. I'm not sure whether to send you to Heaven or Hell! After all, you helped society enormously by putting a computer in almost every home in the world and yet you created that ghastly Windows. I'm going to do something I've never done before. I'm going to let you decide where you want to go!"

Mr. Gates replied, "Well, thanks, Lord. What's the difference between the two?"

God said, "You can take a peek at both places briefly if it will help you decide. Shall we look at Hell first?" "Sure!" said Bill. "Let's go!"

Bill was amazed! He saw a clean, white sandy beach with clear waters. There were thousands of beautiful women running around, playing in the water, laughing and frolicking about.

The sun was shining and the temperature was just perfect!

Bill said, "This is great! If this is Hell, I can't wait to see Heaven!"

To which God replied, "Let's go!" and off they went. Bill saw puffy white clouds in a beautiful blue sky with angels drifting about playing harps and singing.

It was nice, but surely not as enticing as Hell. Mr. Gates thought for only a brief moment and rendered his decision.

"God, I do believe I would like to go to Hell."

"As you desire," said God.

"Oh, THAT!" said God. "That was the screen saver"

****

An American tourist in London decides to skip his tour group and explore the city on his own. He wanders around, seeing the sights, and occasionally stopping at a quaint pub to soak up the local culture, chat with the lads, and have a pint of beer. After a while, he finds himself in a very high-class neighborhood with big. Stately residences---no pubs, no stores, no restaurants, and worst of all, no public restrooms. He really, really has to go, especially after all those beers.

He finds a narrow side-street, with high walls surrounding the adjacent buildings and decides to use the wall to solve his problem. As he is unzipping, he is tapped on the shoulder by a London Bobbie, who says, "I say sir, you simply cannot do that here, you know".

"I'm very sorry officer" he replies, but I really, really have to go and I cannot find a public restroom.

"Ah, yes" said the Bobbie, just follow me" He leads him to a back delivery alley, then along a wall to a gate, which he opens. "In there “points the Bobbie" whizz away anywhere you want" The American enters and finds himself in the most beautiful garden he has ever seen. Manicured grass lawns, statuary, fountains, sculptured hedges, and huge beds of gorgeous flowers, all in perfect bloom.

Since he has the cop's blessing, he unburdens himself and is greatly relieved. As he goes back through the gate, he says to the Bobbie, "that was really decent of you, is that British hospitality?" "No" replies the Bobbie, with a satisfied smile on his face, "That is the French Embassy".

****

Grandma & Grandpa

Grandma and Grandpa were visiting their kids overnight.

When Grandpa found a bottle of Viagra in his son's medicine cabinet, He asked about using one of the pills.

The son said, "I don't think you should take one, Dad; they're very strong and very expensive."

"How much?" asked Grandpa.

"$10 a pill," Answered the son.

"I don't care," said Grandpa, "I'd still like to try one, and before we, Leave in the morning, will put the money under the pillow."

Later the next morning, the son found $110 under the pillow.

He called Grandpa and said, "I told you each pill was $10, not $110.

"I know," said Grandpa. "The $100 is from the Grandma!"

****

An elderly lady was invited to an old friend's home for dinner one evening.

She was impressed by the way her lady friend preceded every request to her husband with endearing terms such as: Honey, My Love, Darling, Sweetheart, etc. The couple had been married almost 70 years and, clearly, they were still very much in love. While the husband was in the living room, her lady friend leaned over to her hostess to say, 'I think it's wonderful that, after all these years, you still call your husband all those loving names'.

The elderly lady hung her head. 'I have to tell you the truth,' she said, 'his name slipped my mind about 10 years ago, and I'm scared to death to ask the cranky old asshole what it is.'

****

The Bottle of Wine

For all of us who are married, were married, wish you were married, or wish you weren't married, this is something to smile about the next time you see a bottle of wine:

Sally was driving home from one of her business trips in Northern Arizona when she saw an elderly Navajo woman walking on the side of the road.

As the trip was a long and quiet one, she stopped the car and asked the Navajo woman if she would like a ride.

With a silent nod of thanks, the woman got into the car.

Resuming the journey, Sally tried in vain to make a bit of small talk with the Navajo woman. The old woman just sat silently, looking intently at everything she saw, studying every little detail, until she noticed a brown bag on the seat next to Sally.

'What in bag?' asked the old woman?

Sally looked down at the brown bag and said, 'It's bottle of wine. I got it for my husband.'

The Navajo woman was silent for another moment or two. Then speaking with the quiet wisdom of an elder, she said:

'Good trade.....'

****

A mother passing by her son's bedroom was astonished to see the bed was nicely made, and everything was picked up. Then, she saw an envelope, propped up prominently on the pillow.

It was addressed, 'Mum'. With the worst premonition, she opened the envelope and read the letter, with trembling hands.

'Dear, Mum.

It is with great regret and sorrow that I'm writing you. I had to elope with my new girlfriend, because I wanted to avoid a scene with Dad and you.

I've been finding real passion with Stacy, and she is so nice, but I knew you would not approve of her, because of all her piercings, tattoos, her tight Motorcycle clothes, and because she is so much older than I am.

But it's not only the passion, Mum. She's pregnant.

Stacy said that we will be very happy. She owns a trailer in the woods, and has a stack of firewood for the whole winter. We share a dream of having many more children.

Stacy has opened my eyes to the fact that marijuana doesn't really hurt anyone. We'll be growing it for ourselves, and trading it with the other people in the commune, for all the cocaine and ecstasy we want.

In the meantime, we'll pray that science will find a cure for AIDS, so Stacy can get better. She sure deserves it!!

Don't worry Mum, I'm 15, and I know how to take care of myself. Someday, I'm sure we'll be back to visit, so you can get to know your many grandchildren.

Love, your son, Nicholas.

PS: Mum, none of the above is true. I'm over at Jason's house.

I just wanted to remind you that there are worse things in life than the school report that's on my desk.

I love you! Call when it is safe for me to come home

Heart Attack

A man suffered a serious heart attack while shopping in a store. The store clerks called 911 when they saw him collapse to the floor. The paramedics rushed the man to the nearest hospital where he had emergency open heart bypass surgery.

He awakened from the surgery to find himself in the care of nuns at the Catholic Hospital he was taken to. A nun was seated next to his bed holding a clip board loaded with several forms, and a pen. She asked him how he was going to pay for his treatment.

"Do you have health insurance?" she asked.

He replied in a raspy voice, "No health insurance."

The nun became agitated and announced loudly, "Nuns are not spinsters! Nuns are married to God."

The patient replied, "Perfect. Send the bill to my brother-in-law."

****

Little boy Goes to his father and asks 'Daddy, how was I born?'

The father Answers, 'Well, son, I guess one day you will need to find out anyway! Your Mom and I first got together in a chat room on Yahoo.

Then I set up a date via e-mail with your Mom and we met at a cyber-cafe. We Sneaked into a secluded room and goggled each other.

There your mother agreed to a download from my hard drive. As soon as I was ready to upload, we discovered that neither one of us had used a firewall, nor since it was too late to hit the delete button, nine months later a little Pop-Up appeared that

Said:

You've got

Male!

****

Think before you speak....

Here are six reasons why you should think before you speak -the last one is great!

Have you ever spoken and wished that you could immediately take the words back...

Here are the Testimonials of a few people who did....

FIRST TESTIMONY:

I walked into a hair salon with my husband and three kids in tow and asked loudly,

'How much do you charge for a shampoo and a blow job?' I turned around and walked back out and never went back

My husband didn't say a word...he knew better.

SECOND TESTIMONY:

I was at the golf store comparing different kinds of golf balls. I was unhappy with the women's type I had been using. After browsing for several minutes, I was approached by one of the good-looking gentlemen who works at the store.

He asked if he could help me.

Without thinking, I looked at him and said, 'I think I like playing with men's balls'

THIRD TESTIMONY:

My sister and I were at the mall and passed by a store that sold a variety of candy and nuts. As we were looking at the display case, the boy behind the counter asked if we needed any help. I replied, 'No, I'm just looking at your nuts.'

My sister started to laugh hysterically.

The boy grinned, and I turned beet-red and walked away.

To this day, my sister has never let me forget.

FOURTH TESTIMONY:

While in line at the bank one afternoon, my toddler decided to release some pent-up energy and ran amok.

I was finally able to grab hold of Her after receiving looks of disgust

And annoyance from other patrons...

I told her that if she did not start behaving 'right now' she would be punished.

To my horror, she looked me in the eye and said in a voice just as threatening,

'If you don't let me go right now, I will tell Grandma that I saw you Kissing Daddy's pee-pee last night!'

The silence was deafening after this enlightening exchange. Even the tellers stopped what they were doing. I mustered up the last of my dignity and walked out of the bank with my daughter in tow.

The last thing I heard when the door closed behind me, were screams of laughter.

FIFTH TESTIMONY:

Have you ever asked your child a question too many times?

My three-year-old son had a lot of problems with potty training and I was on him constantly. One day we stopped at Taco Bell for a quick lunch, in between errands it was very busy, with a full dining room. While enjoying my taco,

I smelled something funny, so of course I checked my seven-month-old daughter, and she was clean.

The realized that Danny Had not asked to go potty in a while.

I asked him if he needed to go, and he said 'No'.

I kept thinking

'Oh Lord, that child has had an accident, and I don't have any clothes with me.'

Then I said, 'Danny, are you SURE you didn't have an accident?'

'No,' he replied.

I just KNEW that he must have had an accident, because the smell was getting worse.

S oooooo, I asked one more time, 'Danny did you have an accident? This time he jumped up, yanked down his pants, Bent over, spread his cheeks

And yelled

'SEE MOM, IT'S JUST FARTS!!'

While 30 people nearly choked to death on their tacos laughing, He calmly pulled up his pants and sat down.

An old couple made me feels better, thanking me for the best laugh they'd ever had!

****

LAST BUT NOT LEAST TESTIMONY:

This had most of the state of Michigan laughing for 2 days and a very embarrassed female news anchor who will, in the future, likely think before she speaks. What happens when you predict snow but don't get any! We had a female news anchor that, the day after it was supposed to have snowed and didn't,

Turned to the weatherman and asked: 'So Bob, where's that 8 inches you Promised me last night?'

Not only did HE have to leave the set, but half the crew did too they were laughing so hard!

****

A Gujrati, a Madrasi and a sardaar were doing construction work on scaffolding on the 20th floor of a building.

They were having lunch and Gujju opened his lunch box & said, "Dhokla ! If I get dhokla one more time for lunch, I'm going to jump off this building."

The Madrasi opened his lunch box and exclaimed, "Idli Sambhar again! If I get idli sambhar one more time I'm going to jump off too."

The sardaar opened his lunch and said, "Parontha again! If I get a parontha one more time, I'm jumping too."

The next day, the Gujju opened his lunch box, saw dhokla, and jumped to his death.

The Madrasi opened his lunch, saw idli sambhar, and jumped, too.

The sardaar opened his lunch, saw the parontha and jumped to his death as well.

At the funeral, Gujju's wife was weeping. She said, "If I'd known how really tired he was of dhokla, I never would have given it to him again!"

The Madrasi's wife also wept and said, "I could have given him dossa! Ididn't realize he hated idli sambhar so much."

Everyone turned and stared at the sardaar's wife.

The sardaar's wife said,

"Don't look at me.

He makes his own lunch."

The Candle Of Love, Hope & Friendship

****

An Italian Boy's Confession

'Bless me Father, for I have sinned. I have been with a loose girl'.

The priest asks, 'Is that you, little Joey Pagano ?'

'Yes, Father, it is.'

'And who was the girl you were with?'

'I can't tell you, Father. I don't want to ruin her reputation'.

"Well, Joey, I'm sure to find out her name sooner or later so you may as well tell me now. Was it Tina Minetti?'

'I cannot say.'

'Was it Teresa Mazzarelli?'

'I'll never tell.'

'Was it Nina Capelli?'

'I'm sorry, but I cannot name her.'

'Was it Cathy Piriano?'

'My lips are sealed.'

'Was it Rosa DiAngelo, then?'

'Please, Father, I cannot tell you.'

The priest sighs in frustration.

'You're very tight lipped, and I admire that. But you've sinned and have to atone. You cannot be an altar boy now for 4 months. Now you go and behave yourself.'

Joey walks back to his pew, and his friend Franco slides over and whispers, 'What'd you get?'

'Four months' vacation and five good leads.'

****

THIS IS THE BEST ONE I HAVE HEARD FOR YEARS; MAYBE AS I AM RE-BORN! INDIAN

Did you ever wonder why Indians are re-born ... well the mystery is now solved..

The angel Gabriel came to the Lord and said 'I have to talk to you. We have Some Indians up here in heaven and they are causing problems. They're Swinging on the pearly gates, my horn is missing, they are wearing Dolce and Gabana saris instead of their white robes, they are riding Mercedes and BMW's instead of the chariots, and they're selling their halos to people for discounted prices. They refuse to keep the stairway to Heaven clear, since they keep crouching down midway eating samosas and drinking chai. Some of them are even walking around with just one wing!'

The Lord said, 'Indians are Indians. Heaven is home to all my children. If

You want to know about real problems, give Satan a call.'

Satan answered the phone, 'Hello? Damn, hold on a minute.' Satan returned to the phone, 'OK I'm back. What can I do for you?'

Gabriel replied, 'I just wanted to know what kind of problems you're having down there.'

Satan says, 'Hold on again. I need to check on something.'

After about 5 minutes Satan returns to the phone and said, 'I'm back. Now what was the question?'

Gabriel said, 'What kind of problems are you having down there?'

Satan says, 'Man, I don't believe this.. Hold on.'

This time Satan was gone at least 15 minutes. He returned and said, "I'm sorry Gabriel, I can't talk right now. These Indians are trying to install air conditioning and making hell a comfortable place to live in by putting out the fire. Fire is there to keep them uncomfortably hot!! Since they are so tech savvy, they were trying to start a telephone connection between heaven and hell. I am having such a hard time controlling and dealing with

Them!! Some were trying to start a chai - pakora shop, which I had to stop. I am requesting Lord to send them back on earth as soon as they arrive as re-birth".

Indians will be Indians.

So this is the story why Indians are re-born!!!

****

A bit of humor for a change.

An Arab needed a heart transplant, but prior to the surgery the doctors needed to store his blood type in case the need arises.

Because the gentleman had a rare type of blood, it couldn't be found locally. So the call went out to a number of countries.

Finally, a Jew was located who had the same blood type and who was willing to donate his blood to the Arab.

After the surgery, the Arab sent the Jew a thank-you card for giving his blood along with an expensive diamond and a new Rolls Royce car as a token of his appreciation. Unfortunately, the Arab had to go through a corrective surgery once again. His doctors called the Jew who was more than happy to donate his blood again. After the second surgery, the Arab sent the Jew a Thank You card and a box of Almond Roca sweets.

The Jew was shocked to see that the Arab this time did not acknowledge the Jew's kind gesture in the same way as he had done the first time. So he phoned the Arab and asked him why he had expressed his appreciation in not a very generous manner.

The Arab replied: "Ya Habibi !!, (Dear

Friend) you have to remember, there is Jewish blood in me now!"

****

The value of a Catholic education and a pencil (this is very cute) you don't even have to be Catholic to appreciate this one.

Little Mary Margaret was not the best student in Catholic School Usually she slept through the class.

One day her teacher, a Nun, called on her while she was sleeping. 'Tell me Mary Margaret, who created the universe?'

When Mary Margaret didn't stir, little Johnny who was her friend sitting behind her, took his pencil and jabbed her in the rear.

'God Almighty!' shouted Mary Margaret.

The Nun said, 'Very good' and continued teaching her class.

A little later the Nun asked Mary Margaret, 'Who is our Lord and Savior?'

But Mary didn't stir from her slumber.

Once again, Johnny came to her rescue and stuck Mary Margaret in the butt.

'Jesus Christ!!!' shouted Mary Margaret and the Nun once again said, 'Very good,' and Mary Margaret fell back sleep.

The Nun asked her a third question...'What did Eve say to Adam after she had her twenty-third child?' Again, Johnny came to the rescue.

This time Mary Margaret jumped up and shouted, 'If you stick that damn thing in me one more time, I'll break it in half!'

The nun fainted.

****

Chinese Name confusion

Caller: Hello, can I speak to Annie Wan ?

Operator: Yes, you can speak to me.

Caller: No, I want to speak to Annie Wan!

Operator: Yes I understand you want to speak to anyone. You can speak to me. Who is this?

Caller: I'm Sam Wan. And I need to talk to Annie Wan! It's urgent.

Operator: I know you are someone and you want to talk to anyone! But what's this urgent matter about?

Caller: Well... just tell my sister Annie Wan that our brother Noe Wan was involved in an accident. Noe Wan got injured and now Noe Wan is being sent to the hospital. Right now, Avery Wan is on his way to the hospital.

Operator: Look, if no one was injured and no one was sent to the hospital, then the accident isn't an urgent matter! You may find this hilarious but I don't have time for this!

Caller: You are so rude! Who are you?

Operator: I'm Saw Ree .

Caller: Yes! You should be sorry. Now give me your name!!

Operator: That's what I said. I'm Saw Ree .

Caller: Oh .....God.... ...

****

Imponderables

1. If you take an Oriental person and spin him around several times, does he become disoriented?

2. If people from Poland are called Poles, why aren't people from Holland called Holes?

3. Do infants enjoy infancy as much as adults enjoy adultery?

4. If a pig loses its voice, is it disgruntled?

5. If love is blind, why is lingerie so popular?

6. Why is the man who invests all your money, called a broker?

7. When cheese gets its picture taken, what does it say?

8. Why is a person who plays the piano called a pianist but a person who drives a racing car not called a racist?

9. Why are a wise man and, a wise guy, opposites?

10. Why does overlook and oversee mean opposite things?

11. Why isn't the number 11 pronounced onety-one?

12. "I am" is reportedly the shortest sentence in the English language... Could it be that "I do" is the longest sentence?

13. If lawyers are disbarred and clergymen defrocked, doesn't it follow that electricians can be delighted, musicians denoted, cowboys deranged, models deposed, tree surgeons debarked, and dry cleaners depressed?

14. What hair color do they put on the driver's licenses of bald men?

15. I thought about how mothers feed their babies with tiny little spoons and forks, so I wondered what Chinese mothers use. Toothpicks?

16. Why do they put pictures of criminals up in the Post Office? What are we supposed to do, write to

them? Why don't they just put their pictures on the postage stamps so the postmen can look for them while they deliver the mail?

17. You never really learn to swear until you learn to drive.

18. No one ever says, "It's only a game," when their team is winning.

19. Isn't making a smoking section in a restaurant like making a peeing section in a swimming pool?

20.OK... so if the Jacksonville Jaguars are known as the 'Jags' and the Tampa Bay Buccaneers are known as the 'Bucs,' what does that make the Tennessee Titans?

21. Why if you send something by road it is called a shipment, but when you send it by sea it is called cargo?

22. If a convenience store is open 24 hours a day, 7 days a week, 365 days a year, why are there locks on the door?

****

A stranger was seated next to an 8-year old girl on the airplane when the stranger turned to her and said, 'Let's talk, I've heard that flights go quicker if you strike up a conversation with your fellow passenger.

The little girl, who had just opened her book, closed it slowly and said to the stranger, 'what would you like to talk about?'

'Oh, I don't know,' said the stranger 'How about nuclear power? And he smiles.

'OK,' she said. 'That could be an interesting topic. But let me ask you a question first. A horse, a cow, and a deer all eat the same stuff - grass - Yet a deer excretes little pellets, while a cow turns out a flat patty, and a horse produces clumps of dried grass. Why do you suppose that is?'

The stranger, visibly surprised by the little girl's intelligence, thinks about it and says, 'Hmmm, I have no idea.'

To which the little girl replies, 'Do you really feel qualified to discuss nuclear power when you don't know shit?

****

The Pastor's Ass

The pastor entered his donkey in a race and it won. The pastor was so pleased with the donkey that he entered it in the race again, and it won again.

The local paper read: PASTOR'S ASS OUT FRONT

The Bishop was so upset with this kind of publicity that he ordered the pastor not to enter the donkey in another race.

The next day, the local paper headline read: BISHOP SCRATCHES PASTOR'S ASS

This was too much for the bishop, so he ordered the pastor to get rid of the donkey.

The pastor decided to give it to a nun in a nearby convent.

The local paper, hearing of the news, posted the following headline the next day: NUN HAS BEST ASS IN TOWN the bishop fainted.

He informed the nun that she would have to get rid of the donkey, so she sold it to a farmer for $10.

The next day the paper read: NUN SELLS ASS FOR $10

This was too much for the bishop, so he ordered the nun to buy back the donkey and lead it to the plains where it could run wild.

The next day the headlines read: NUN ANNOUNCES HER ASS IS WILD AND FREE the bishop was buried the next day.

The moral of the story is....being concerned about public opinion can bring you much grief and misery...and even shorten your life. So be yourself and enjoy life...Stop worrying about everyone else's ass and you'll be a lot happier and live longer! Have a wonderful day!

****

About a century or two ago, the Pope decided that all the Sikhs had to leave Italy. Naturally there was a big uproar from the Sikh community. So the Pope made a deal. He would have a religious debate with a member of the Sikh community. If the Sikh won, the Sikhs could stay. If the Pope won, the Sikhs would leave. The Sikhs realized that they had no choice so they picked a middle-aged man named Harbinder Singh to represent them.

Harbinder asked for one additional condition to the debate to make it more interesting, neither side would be allowed to talk.

The Pope agreed.

The day of the great debate came.

Harbinder Singh and the Pope sat opposite each other for a full minute.

Then the Pope raised his hand and showed three fingers.

Harbinder looked back at him and raised one finger.

The Pope waved his fingers in a circle around his head.

Harbinder pointed to the ground where he sat.

The Pope pulled out a wafer and a glass of wine.

Harbinder pulled out an apple.

The Pope stood up and said, 'I give up. This man is too good. The Sikhs can stay.'

An hour later, the cardinals were gathered around the Pope asking him what had happened.

The Pope said, 'First I held up three fingers to represent the holy trinity. He responded by holding up one finger to remind me that there was still One God common to both our religions.

Then, I waved my finger around me to show him that God was all around us. He responded by pointing to the ground and showing that God was also right here with us.

Then, I pulled out the wine and wafer to show that God absolves us from our sins. He pulled out an apple to remind me of original sin.

He had an answer for everything. What could I do?'

Meanwhile, the Sikh community had crowded around Harbinder Singh.

'What happened?' they asked.

'Well,' said Harbinder, 'First he said to me that the Sikhs had three days to get out of here.

I told him not one of us was leaving.

Then he told me that this whole city would be cleared of Sikhs.

I let him know that we were staying right here.'

'Yes, and then???' Asked the crowd.

'I don't know', said Harbinder,

'He took out his lunch, so I took out mine!!

****

Wedding Ceremony

Everyone in the wedding ceremony was watching the radiant bride as her father escorted her down the aisle to give away to the groom.

They reached the altar and the waiting groom; the bride kissed her father and placed something in his hand.

Everyone in the room was wondering what was given to the father by the bride.

The father could feel the suspense in the air and all eyes were on him to divulge the secret and say something.

So he announced 'Ladies and Gentlemen today is the luckiest day of my life.'

Then he raised his hands with what his daughter gave him and continued, 'My daughter finally, finally returned my credit card to me.'

The whole audience including priest started laughing....But not the poor groom!

****

A young unmarried girl discovers that she is pregnant. Scared, she confides

This ' news' to her mother. Shouting, cursing, crying, the mother says, "Who was the pig that did this to you? I want to know!" The girl picks up the phone and makes a call.

Half an hour later a Ferrari stops in front of their house; a mature and distinguished man with gray hair and impeccably dressed in a very expensive suit steps out of it and enters the house.

He sits in the living room with the father, the mother and the Girl, and tells them: "Good morning, your daughter has informed me of the problem. However, I can't marry her because of my personal family situation, but I'll take responsibility.

If a girl is born I will bequeath her 2 retail stores, a townhouse, a beach villa and a $1,000,000 bank account.

If a boy is born, my legacy will be a couple of factories and a $2,000,000bank account.

If it is twins, a factory and $1,000,000 each. However, if there is a miscarriage or unsuccessful delivery, what do you suggest I do?"

At this point, the father, who had remained silent, places a hand firmly on the man's shoulder and tells him, "You can try again!..............."

****

Simple clean Parsi humor.....

Hosi's dad used to put his thumb impression on his mark sheets, progress reports, remarks diary etc...

One day Hosi asked his father:

Being a Chartered Accountant, why are you putting your thumb impression, instead of signing on my mark sheets, progress cards, remarks register?

Hosi's dad replied:

Ghelo, after looking at your marks, the teacher should not think that I am educated....

****

You know you are living in 2021 when..............

1. You pull up in your own driveway and use your cell phone to see if anyone is home to help you carry in the groceries.

2. You haven't played solitaire with real cards in years.

3. You have a list of 15 phone numbers to reach your family of three.

4. You e-mail the person who works at the desk next to you.

5. Your reason for not staying in touch with friends and family is that they don't have e-mail addresses.

6. You accidentally enter your password on the microwave.

7. Every commercial on television has a web site at the bottom of the screen.

8. Leaving the house without your cell phone, which you didn't have the first 20 or 30 (or 0) years of your life, is now a cause for panic and you turn around to go and get it.

10. You get up in the morning and go on line before getting your coffee.

11. You're reading this and nodding and laughing.

12. Even worse, you know exactly to whom you are going to forward this message.

13. You are too busy to notice there was no #9 on this list.

14. You actually scrolled back up to check that there wasn't a #9 on this list.

AND NOW U R LAUGHING at yourself.

****

Three men, recently married, were sitting together over a beer and mostly bragging about how they had fared while briefing their wives on what they expected of them by way of performing marital duties.

The first man had married a Bengali girl -- of eastern orientation in India -- and bragged that he had told his wife she was going to do all the dishes and house cleaning. He said it took a couple of days, but by the third day the dishes were done.

The second man had married a Tamil girl – of southern persuasion .He bragged that he had given his wife orders that she was to do all the cleaning, doing dishes as well as the cooking. On the first day he didn't see any results, but the next day it was better. By the third day, his house was clean, the dishes were done and he had a huge dinner laid out on the table.

The third man had married a Punjabi girl – of Northern Province. He boasted that he, too, had told his wife that her duty was to keep the house clean, dishes washed, lawn mowed, laundry done and an exciting new meal on the table every day. He said the first day he didn't see anything, the second day he didn't see anything either but by the third day most of the swelling had gone down and he could see a little out of his left eye.....

****

A man, his wife, and mother-in-law went on vacation to the Holy Land. While they were there, the mother-in-law passed away suddenly. The local undertaker told them, "You can have her shipped home for $5,000, or you can bury her here in the Holy Land for $150.00."

The man thought about it and decided to have the mother-in-law shipped home.

The undertaker asked, "Why would you spend $5,000 to ship your mother-in-law home, when it would cost only $150.00 to bury her here?"

The man replied, "A man died here 2000 years ago, was buried here, and three days later he rose from the dead. I just can't take that chance."

****

A couple in their nineties are both having problems remembering things, so they decide to go to the doctor for a checkup.

The doctor tells them that they're physically okay, but they might want to start writing things down to help them remember.

Later that night, while watching TV, the old man gets up from his chair.

His wife asks, "Where are you going?"

"To the kitchen" he replies.

"Will you get me a bowl of ice cream?"

"Sure."

"Don't you think you should write it down so you can remember it?" she asks.

"No, I can remember it."

"Well, I'd like some strawberries on top, too. You'd better write it down because you know you'll forget it."

He says, "I can remember that! You want a bowl of ice cream with strawberries."

"I'd also like whipped cream. I'm certain you'll forget that, so you'd better write it down!" she retorts.

Irritated, he says, "I don't need to write it down, I can remember it! Leave me alone! Ice cream with strawberries and whipped cream - I got it, for goodness sake!" Then he grumbles into the kitchen.

After about 20 minutes the old man returns from the kitchen and hands his wife a plate of bacon and eggs.

She stares at the plate for a moment and says - "Where's my toast?

Keep Reading

A senior citizen said to his eighty-year old buddy: "So I hear you're getting married?"

"Yep!"

"Do I know her?"

"Nope!"

"This woman, is she good looking?"

“Not really."

“Is she a good cook?"

"Naw, she can't cook too well."

"Does she have lots of money?"

"Nope! Poor as a church

Mouse."

"Well then, is she good in bed?"

"I don't know."

"Why in the world do you want to marry her then?"

"Because, she can still drive!"

Keep Reading

Three old guys are out walking.

First one says, "Windy, isn't it?"

Second one says, "No, it's Thursday!"

Third one says, "So am I. Let's go get a beer."

Keep Reading

A man was telling his neighbor, "I just bought a new hearing aid. It cost me four thousand dollars, but its state of the art. It's perfect."

"Really," answered the neighbor. "What kind is it?"

"Twelve thirty."

Keep Reading

Morris, an 82 year-old man, went to the doctor to get a physical.

A few days later the doctor saw Morris walking down the street with a gorgeous young woman on his arm.

A couple of days later the doctor spoke to Morris and said, "You're really doing great, aren't you?"

Morris replied, "Just doing what you said, Doc. 'Get a hot mamma and be cheerful.'"

The doctor said, "I didn't say that. I said, 'You've got a heart murmur .Be careful.'"

Keep Reading

A little old man shuffled slowly into an ice cream parlor and pulled himself slowly, painfully, up onto a stool.

After catching his breath, he ordered a banana split. The waitress asked kindly, "Crushed nuts?"

"No," he replied, "arthritis."

****

Marriage proposal

Madam:

I am an olden young uncle living only with myself in Bangaloru. Having seen your advertisement for marriage purposes, I decided to press myself on you and hope you will take me nicely.

I am a soiled son from inside Karnataka. I am nice and big, six foot tall and six inches long. My body is filled with hardness, as because I am working hardly. I am playing hardly also. Especially I like cricket and I am a good batter and I am fast baller. Whenever I come running in for balling, other batters start running. Everybody is scared of my rapid balls that bounce a lot. I am very nice man. I am always laughing loudly at everyone. I am jolly.

I am gay.

Especially ladies, they are saying I am nice and soft. I am always giving respect to the ladies. I am always allowing ladies to get on top.

That is how nice I am.

I am not having any bad habits. I am not drinking and I am not sucking tobacco or anything else. Every morning I am going to the gym and I am pumping like anything. Daily I am pumping and pumping. If you want, you can come and see how much I am pumping the dumb belles in the gym. I am having a lot of money in my pants and my pants is always open for you. I am such a nice man, but still I am living with myself only. What to do? So

I am taking things into my own hands every day. That is why I am pressing myself on you, so that you will come in my house and take my things into your hand.

If you are marrying me madam, I am telling you, I will love you very hard every day. In fact, I will stop pumping dumb belles in the gym.

If you are not marrying me madam and not coming to me, I will press you and press you until you come. So I am placing my head between your nicely smelling feet and looking up with lots of hope. I am waiting very badly for your reply and I am stiff with anticipation.

Expecting soon.

****

A Mother had 3 virgin daughters and they were all getting married within a short time period. Because Mom was a bit worried about how their sex life would get started, she made them all promise to send a postcard from the honeymoon with a few words on how marital sex felt.

The first girl sent a card from Hawaii two days after the wedding. The card said nothing but "Nescafe." Mom was puzzled at first, but then went to the kitchen and got out the Nescafe jar. It said: "Good till the last drop."

Mom blushed, but was pleased for her daughter.

The second girl sent the card from Vermont a week after the wedding, and the card read: "Benson & Hedges". Mom now knew to go straight to her husband's cigarettes, and she read from the Benson & Hedges pack: "Extra-long. King Size.

She was again slightly embarrassed but still happy for her daughter.

The third girl left for her honeymoon in the Caribbean. Mom waited for a week, nothing. Another week went by and still nothing. Then after a whole month, a card finally arrived. Written on it with shaky handwriting were the words "British Airways." Mom took out her latest Harper's Bazaar magazine, flipped through the pages fearing the worst, and finally found the ad for BA. The ad said: "Three times a day, seven days a week, both ways."

Mom fainted...

****

NUDITY

I was driving with my three young children one warm summer evening when a Woman in the convertible ahead of us stood up and waved. She was stark naked! As I was reeling from the shock, I heard my 5-year-old shout from the back seat, "Mom! That lady isn't wearing a seat belt!

OPINIONS

On the first day of school, a first-grader handed his teacher a Note from his mother. The note read, "The opinions expressed by this child are not necessarily those of his parents."

MORE NUDITY

A little boy got lost at the YMCA and found himself in the women's locker room. When he was spotted, the room burst into shrieks, with ladies grabbing towels and running for cover. The little boy watched in amazement and then asked!!! "What's the matter haven't you ever seen a little boy before?"

****

ELDERLY

While working for an organization that delivers lunches to elderly shut-ins, I used to take my 4-year-old daughter on my afternoon rounds. The various appliances of old age, particularly the canes, walkers and wheelchairs, unfailingly intrigued her. One day I found her staring at a pair of false teeth soaking in a glass. As I braced myself for the inevitable barrage of questions, she merely turned and whispered, "The tooth fairy will never believe this!"

SCHOOL

A little girl had just finished her first week of school. "I'm just wasting my time," she said to her mother. "I can't read, I can't write and they won't let me talk!"

BIBLE

A little boy opened the big family bible. He was fascinated as he fingered through the old pages. Suddenly, something fell out of the Bible. He picked up the object and looked at it. What he saw was an old leaf that had been pressed in between the pages. "Mama, look what I found", the boy called out." What have you got there, dear?" With astonishment in the young boy's voice, he answered, "I think it's Adam's underwear."

Two men sat in a bar drinking.

First man: I have family troubles, so to this the second replied: Why don't you first listen to mine.

"I married a widow with a young daughter. The trouble started when my father married my daughter.

My daughter became my mother and thus my wife my grandmother".

"Further trouble started when I had a son.

My son is my father brother thus my uncle".

"Situation turned worse when my father had a son.

Now my father's son, who is now my brother, is also my grandson".

"Ultimately I have become my own grandfather and my own grandson".

!!??And then you say you have family problems!!??

****

Mary had a little pig, she kept it fat and plastered;

And when the price of pork went up, she shot the little bastard.

MARY HAD A LITTLE LAMB

Her father shot it dead. Now it goes to school with her,

Between two hunks of bread.

JACK AND JILL went up the hill

To have a little fun.

Stupid Jill forgot the pill

And now they have a son.

SIMPLE SIMON met a pie man going to the fair.

Said Simple Simon to the pie man

"What have you got there?"

Said the pie man unto Simon,

"Pies, you dumb #$%!"

HUMPTY DUMPTY sat on a wall,

Humpty Dumpty had a great fall.

All the kings' horses,

And all the kings' men.

Had scrambled eggs,

For breakfast again.

HEY DIDDLE, DIDDLE the cat took a piddle,

All over the bedside clock.

The little dog laughed to see such fun.

Then died of electric shock.

GEORGIE PORGY Pudding and Pie,

Kissed the girls and made them cry.

And when the boys came out to play,

He kissed them too 'cause he was gay.

There was a little girl who had a little curl

Right in the middle of her forehead.

When she was good, she was very, very good.

But when she was bad........

She got a fur coat, jewels, a waterfront condo, and a sports car.

****

WHO DOES WHAT

A man and his wife were having an argument about who should brew the coffee each morning.

The wife said, "You should do it, because you get up first, and then we don't have to wait as long to get our coffee."

The husband said, "You are in charge of cooking around here and you should do it, because that is your job, and I can just wait for my coffee."

Wife replies, "No, you should do it, and besides, it is in the Bible that the man should do the coffee."

Husband replies, "I can't believe that, show me." So she fetched the Bible, and opened the New Testament and showed him at the top of several pages, that it indeed says..... HEBREWS

****

WHEN I'M 100, IF I LEAN A LITTLE. LET ME!

The family wheeled Grandma out on the lawn, in her wheelchair, where the activities for her 100th birthday were taking place. Grandma couldn't speak very well, but she could write notes when she needed to communicate.

After a short time out on the lawn, Grandma started leaning off to the right, so some family members grabbed her, straightened her up, and stuffed pillows on her right.

A short time later, she started leaning off to her left, so again the family grabbed her and stuffed pillows on her left.

Soon she started leaning forward, so the family members again grabbed her, and then tied a pillowcase around her waist to hold her up.

A nephew who arrived late came up to Grandma and said, "Hi, Grandma, you're looking good! How are they treating you?"

Grandma took out her little notepad and slowly wrote a note to the nephew.

"They won't let me fart."

****

Three sons left home, started careers and prospered.

Getting back together, they discussed the gifts that they were able to give their elderly mother for her seventieth birthday.

The first said, "I built a big house for Mom."

The second said, "I sent her a Mercedes with a driver."

The third smiled and said, "I've got you both beat. You know how Mom enjoys the Bible and you know she can't see very well. I sent her a brown parrot that can recite the entire Bible. It took 20 monks in a monastery 12 years to teach him. I had to pledge to contribute $100,000 a year for 10 years, but it was worth it. Mom just has to name the chapter and verse and the parrot will recite it."

Soon thereafter, Mom sent out letters of thanks:

She wrote to the first son, "Milton, the house you built is not practical. I live in only one room, but I have to heat, cool, and clean the whole house."

She wrote to the second son, "Marvin, I am too old to travel. I stay home all the time, so I never use the Mercedes. And the driver is so rude!"

She wrote the third son, "Dearest Melvin, you were the only son to have the good sense to know what your mother likes. The chicken was delicious."

****

For his birthday, little Patrick asked for a 10-speedbicycle. His father said, "Son, we'd give you one, but the mortgage on this house is $80,000 & your mother just lost her job. There's no way we can afford it."

The next day the father saw little Patrick heading out the front door with a suitcase. So he asked, "Son, where are you going?"

Little Patrick told him, "I was walking past your room last night heard you telling mom you were pulling out. Then I heard her tell you to wait because she was coming too. And I'll be damned if I'm staying here by myself with an $80,000 mortgage & no bike!"

****

Commandment 1.

Marriages are made in heaven. But so again, are thunder and lightning.

Commandment 2.

If you want your husband to listen and pay strict attention to every word you say, talk in your sleep.

Commandment 3.

Marriage is grand -- and divorce is at least 100 grand!

Commandment 4.

Married life is very frustrating. In the first year of marriage, the man speaks and the woman listens. In the second year, the woman speaks and the man listens. In the third year, they both speak and the neighbors listen.

Commandment 5.

When a man opens the door of his car for his wife, you can be sure of one thing: Either the car is new or the wife is.

Commandment 6.

Marriage is when a man and woman become as one; the trouble starts when they try to decide which one.

Commandment 7.

Before marriage, a man will lie awake all night thinking about something you say. After marriage, he will fall asleep before you finish.

Commandment 8.

Every man wants a wife who is beautiful, understanding, economical, and a good cook. But the law allows only one wife.

Commandment 9.

Marriage and love are purely a matter of chemistry. That is why wife treats husband like toxic waste.

Commandment 10.

A woman is incomplete until she is married. After that, she is finished.

****

GRANDPARENTS' ANSWERING MACHINE!

Good Morning! At present, we are not at home, but please leave your message after you hear the beep. ☼

Beeeeeppp...

- If you are one of our children, dial 1 and then select the option from 1 to 5 in order of "birth arrival" so we know who it is.

- If you need us to stay with the children, press 2.

- If you want to borrow the car, press 3.

- If you want us to wash your clothes and do iron, press 4.

- If you want the grandchildren to sleep here tonight, press 5.

- If you want us to pick up the kids at school, press 6.

- If you want us to prepare a meal for Sunday or to have it delivered to your home, press 7.

• If you want to come to eat here, press 8.

• If you need money, press 9.

• If you are going to invite us to dinner or take us to the theatre, start talking...we are listening!

****

There is a traveling dildo salesman. He knocks on a woman's door and she allows him in. He states: "I have a dildo worth 10 dollars", "another worth 20 dollars", "and another worth 30 dollars".

She looks them over and finally asks him: "How much for the silver dildo?"

He contemplates for a second and says "um...150 dollars." She says: "ok, I'll take it".

He leaves. Later that day he's back at the office and his boss asks him what he sold that day. The salesman replies: "I sold three 10 dollar dildos, seven 20 dollar dildos, two 30 dollar dildos, and I got 150 bucks for my thermos!!

****

A naughty poem!

The Country was in a terrible state,

As the Parliament sat for the Budget Debate.

It was quite a few minutes before Pranab spoke,

Then he said, 'Sex will cost you two bucks a poke,

Whether your short, skinny or thick.

A tax will be paid on the use of your prick'.
Rahul rose and said 'Pranab look here,
Will this tax apply to those who are queer?'
Greenie Gadhkari looked rather glum,
'May I be exempt, I only like bum.'
Pranab replied and sounded quite airy
'You'll pay double you dirty old fairy'

Up rose Jaitly, to tremendous applause
Grabbed Miera and ripped off her drawers
He straddled across her and screwed her at will
Then shouted to Pranab, 'Put that on the Bill'!

Advani shouted, 'I think I'll resign,
I haven't had sex for a very long time.
I dream every night of a big juicy crutch,
But two bucks a go.... That's too bloody much.'

The House was in uproar, the fighting went on,
Till Munda banged on the Bar with his dong,
'With a tax on a poke in the front and the back
All we can do is have a good whack.'
I disagree said Sibal with a leer,
And stuck his big prick into Sushma's ear.

The backbenchers came and the Cabinet went
Manmohan took his out and found it was bent.
'Look here', he cried as it swung in the air,
'For those who are bent a discount is fair.'
So all checked their dicks, the Munda was last,
And in the excitement, the damn Bill was passed.
So now in the beds of India at night,
There's many a fanny that's closed up real tight.
They're taxing our booze and taxing our smokes
And now they are taxing our pokes.
If two bucks a head is the price we must pay
It now with ourselves we find we must play
To quench our frustrations we must have a wank
And for the state of our Country – we've Pranab to thank!

****

A cabbie picks up a Nun.

She gets into the cab, and notices that the VERY handsome cab driver won't stop staring at her. She asks him why he is staring.

He replies: "I have a question to ask you but I don't want to offend you."

She answers, "My son, you cannot offend me. When you're as old as I am and have been a nun as long as I have, you get a chance to see and hear just about everything. I'm sure that there's nothing you could say or ask that I would find offensive."

"Well, I've always had a fantasy to have a nun kiss me."

She responds, "Well, let's see what we can do about that: #1, you have to be single and #2, you must be Catholic."

The cab driver is very excited and says,

"Yes, I'm single and Catholic!"

"OK" the nun says. "Pull into the next alley."

The nun fulfils his fantasy, with a kiss that would make a hooker blush.

But when they get back on the road, the cab driver starts crying.

"My dear child," says the nun, "why are you crying?"

"Forgive me but I've sinned. I lied and I must confess, I'm married and I'm Jewish."

The nun says, "That's OK. My name is Fred and I'm going to a Halloween party."

****

This is a beautiful story. Read the entire story!!!

A Father, Daughter & a Dog - story by Catherine Worthmoore

"Watch out! You nearly broad sided that car!" My father yelled at me. "Can't you do anything right?"

Those words hurt worse than blows. I turned my head toward the elderly man in the seat beside me, daring me to challenge him. A lump rose in my throat as I averted my eyes. I wasn't prepared for another battle.

"I saw the car, Dad. Please don't yell at me when I'm driving."

My voice was measured and steady, sounding far calmer than I really felt.

Dad glared at me, then turned away and settled back. At home I left Dad in front of the television and went outside to collect my thoughts.... dark, heavy clouds hung in the air with a promise of rain. The rumble of distant thunder seemed to echo my inner turmoil. What could I do about him?

Dad had been a lumberjack in Washington and Oregon. He had enjoyed being outdoors and had reveled in pitting his strength against the forces of nature. He had entered grueling lumberjack competitions, and had placed often. The shelves in his house were filled with trophies that attested to his prowess.

The years marched on relentlessly. The first time he couldn't lift a heavy log, he joked about it; but later that same day I saw him outside alone, straining to lift it. He became irritable whenever anyone teased him about his advancing age, or when he couldn't do something he had done as a younger man.

Four days after his sixty-seventh birthday, he had a heart attack. An ambulance sped him to the hospital while a paramedic administered CPR to keep blood and oxygen flowing.

At the hospital, Dad was rushed into an operating room. He was lucky; he survived. But something inside Dad died. His zest for life was gone. He obstinately refused to follow doctor's orders. Suggestions and offers of help were turned aside with sarcasm and insults. The number of visitors thinned, then finally stopped altogether. Dad was left alone

My husband, Dick, and I asked Dad to come live with us on our small farm. We hoped the fresh air and rustic atmosphere would help him adjust.

Within a week after he moved in, I regretted the invitation. It seemed nothing was satisfactory. He criticized everything I did. I became frustrated and moody. Soon I was taking my pent-up anger out on Dick. We began to bicker and argue.

Alarmed, Dick sought out our pastor and explained the situation. The clergyman set up weekly counseling appointments for us. At the close of each session he prayed, asking God to soothe the Dad's troubled mind.

But the months wore on and God was silent. Something had to be done and it was up to me to do it.

The next day I sat down with the phone book and methodically called each of the mental health clinics listed in the Yellow Pages. I explained my problem to each of the sympathetic voices that answered in vain.

Just when I was giving up hope, one of the voices suddenly exclaimed, "I just read something that might help you! Let me go get the article."

I listened as she read. The article described a remarkable study done at a nursing home. All of the patients were under treatment for chronic depression. Yet their attitudes had improved dramatically when they were given responsibility for a dog.

I drove to the animal shelter that afternoon... After I filled out a questionnaire, a uniformed officer led me to the kennels. The odor of disinfectant stung my nostrils as I moved down the row of pens. Each contained five to seven dogs. Long-haired dogs, curly-haired dogs, black dogs, spotted dogs all jumped up, trying to reach me.

I studied each one but rejected one after the other for various reasons too big, too small, too much hair. As I neared the last pen a dog in the shadows of the far corner struggled to his feet, walked to the front of the run and sat down. It was a pointer, one of the dog world's aristocrats. But this was a caricature of the breed.

Years had etched his face and muzzle with shades of gray. His hip bones jutted out in lopsided triangles. But it was his eyes that caught and held my attention. Calm and clear, they beheld me unwaveringly.

I pointed to the dog. "Can you tell me about him?" The officer looked, then shook his head in puzzlement. "He's a funny one. Appeared out of nowhere and sat in front of the gate. We brought him in, figuring someone would be right down to claim him. That was two weeks ago and we've heard nothing. His time is up tomorrow." He gestured helplessly.

As the words sank in I turned to the man in horror.. "You mean you're going to kill him?"

"Ma'am," he said gently, "that's our policy. We don't have room for every unclaimed dog."

I looked at the pointer again. The calm brown eyes awaited my decision. "I'll take him," I said. I drove home with the dog on the front seat beside me.. When I reached the house I honked the horn twice. I was helping my prize out of the car when Dad shuffled onto the front porch... "Ta-da! Look what I got for you, Dad!" I said excitedly.

Dad looked, then wrinkled his face in disgust. "If I had wanted a dog I would have gotten one. And I would have picked out a better specimen than that bag of bones. Keep it! I don't want it" Dad waved his arm scornfully and turned back toward the house.

Anger rose inside me. It squeezed together my throat muscles and pounded into my temples. "You'd better get used to him, Dad. He's staying!"

Dad ignored me. "Did you hear me, Dad?" I screamed. At those words Dad whirled angrily, his hands clenched at his sides, his eyes narrowed and blazing with hate. We stood glaring at each other like duelists, when suddenly the pointer pulled free from my grasp. He wobbled toward my dad and sat down in front of him. Then slowly, carefully, he raised his paw.

Dad's lower jaw trembled as he stared at the uplifted paw Confusion replaced the anger in his eyes. The pointer waited patiently. Then Dad was on his knees hugging the animal.

It was the beginning of a warm and intimate friendship. Dad named the pointer Cheyenne. Together he and Cheyenne explored the community. They spent long hours walking down dusty lanes. They spent reflective moments on the banks of

Streams, angling for tasty trout. They even started to attend Sunday services together, Dad sitting in a pew and Cheyenne lying quietly at is feet.

Dad and Cheyenne were inseparable throughout the next three years... Dad's bitterness faded, and he and Cheyenne made many friends. Then late one night I was startled to feel Cheyenne's cold nose burrowing through our bed covers. He had never before come into our bedroom at night. I woke Dick, put on my robe and ran into my father's room. Dad lay in his bed, his face serene. But his spirit had left quietly sometime during the night.

Two days later my shock and grief deepened when I discovered Cheyenne lying dead beside Dad's bed. I wrapped his still form in the rag rug he had slept on.

As Dick and I buried him near a favorite fishing hole, I silently thanked the dog for the help he had given me in restoring Dad's peace of mind.

The morning of Dad's funeral dawned overcast and dreary. This day looks like the way I feel, I thought, as I walked down the aisle to the pews reserved for family. I was surprised to see the many friends Dad and Cheyenne had made filling the church. The pastor began his eulogy. It was a tribute to both Dad and the dog who had changed his life.

And then the pastor turned to Hebrews 13:2. "Do not neglect to show hospitality to strangers, for by this some have entertained angels without knowing it."

"I've often thanked God for sending that angel," he said.

For me, the past dropped into place, completing a puzzle that I had not seen before: the sympathetic voice that had just read the right article... Cheyenne's unexpected appearance at the animal shelter.. ...his calm acceptance and complete devotion to my father.. And the proximity of their deaths. And suddenly I understood. I knew that God had answered my prayers after all.

****

Life is too short for drama or petty things, so laugh hard, love truly and forgive quickly. Live While You Are Alive. Forgive now those who made you cry. You might not get a second time.

And if you don't send this to at least 4 people ---nobody cares. But do share this with someone. Lost time can never be found

God answers our prayers in His time........not ours.

****

Woman asks:

If I sleep with 3 men, everyone calls me a slut.

But when a man sleeps with 8 girls,

everyone calls him a real man. How come?

Man replies:It's very simple. Confucious say 'When one lock can be opened by 3 different keys, it's a bad key lock.

But when one key can open 8 different locks, we call it a 'master key'.

****

A man boards a flight from Delhi to Mumbai and takes his seat. As he settles in, he glances up and sees a gorgeous woman boarding the plane.

He soon realizes she's heading straight towards his seat. Lo and behold, she takes the seat right next to his.

Eager to strike up a conversation, he asks 'Business trip or vacation? ‘She turns, smiles, and says, 'Business. I'm going to the annual Sexologists Convention.'

He swallows hard. Here is the most gorgeous woman he has ever seen, sitting next to him, and she's a sexologist! Struggling to contain his excitement and maintain his composure, he calmly asks, 'what's your business role at this convention? 'Lecturer,' she says, 'I use my experience to debunk some of the popular myths about sexuality.' 'Really?' he says, swallowing hard. 'What m-m-m-myths are those?' 'Well,' she explains, 'one popular myth is that African men are the best endowed when, in fact, it's the Tamilian who is most likely to possess that trait. Another popular myth is that Frenchmen are the best lovers, whereas actually it is the Bengali... However, we have found that the best potential lover in all categories is Rahul.'

Suddenly, the woman becomes a little uncomfortable and blushes. 'I'm sorry,' she says, 'I shouldn't be discussing this with you.

I don't even know your name!'

'Venkatraman !' the man blurts out. ' Venkatraman Mukherjee ! But all my friends call me Joginder Singh......!!!!!!!!!'

****

After having failed his exam a Student goes and confronts his lecturer about it.

Student: "Sir, do you really understand anything about the subject?"

Professor: "Surely I must. Otherwise I would not be a professor!"

Student: "Great, well then I would like to ask you a question. If you can give me

The correct answer, I will accept my mark as is and go. If you however do not know the answer, I want you give me an

"A" for the Exam. "

Professor: "Okay,

It's a deal. So what is the question?"

Student: "What is legal, but not logical, logical, but not legal, and neither logical, nor legal?"

Even after some long and hard consideration, the professor cannot give the student an answer, and therefore changes his exam mark into an "A", as agreed.

Afterwards, the professor calls on his best student and asks him the same question.

He immediately answers.

"Sir, you are 63 years old and married to a 35 Year old woman, which is legal, but not logical. Your wife has a 25 Year old lover, which is logical, but not legal. The fact that you have given your wife's lover an "A", although he really should have failed, is neither legal, nor logical."

****

On their wedding night, the young bride approached her new husband and asked for $20.00 for their first lovemaking encounter. In his highly aroused state, her husband readily agreed.

This scenario was repeated each time they made love, for more than 30 years, with him thinking that it was a cute way for her to afford new clothes and other incidentals that she needed.

Arriving home around noon one day, she was surprised to find her husband in a very drunken state. During the next few minutes, he explained that his employer was going through a process of corporate downsizing, and he had been let go.

It was unlikely that, at the age of 59, he'd be able to find another job.

Calmly, his wife handed him a bank book which showed more than thirty years of steady deposits and interest totaling nearly$1 million.

Then she showed him certificates of deposits issued by the bank which were worth over $2 million.

She explained that she had 'charged' him for sex, and these were the results of her savings and investments.

The husband was so astounded he could barely speak. Finally he found his voice and blurted out, 'If I'd had any idea at what you were doing, I would have had sex only with you.'

That's when she shot him.

MEN JUST DONT KNOW WHEN TO KEEP THEIR MOUTHS SHUT!!!!!!!!

****

Summary of Life

GREAT TRUTHS THAT LITTLE CHILDREN HAVE LEARNED:

1) No matter how hard you try, you can't baptize cats.

2) When your Mom is mad at your Dad, don't let her brush your hair.

3) If your sister hits you, don't hit her back. They always catch the second person.

4) Never ask your 3-year old brother to hold a tomato.

5) You can't trust dogs to watch your food.

6) Don't sneeze when someone is cutting your hair.

7) Never hold a Dust-Buster and a cat at the same time.

8) You can't hide a piece of broccoli in a glass of milk.

9) Don't wear polka-dot underwear under white shorts.

10) The best place to be when you're sad is Grandpa's lap.

GREAT TRUTHS THAT ADULTS HAVE LEARNED:

1) Raising teenagers is like nailing jelly to a tree.

2) Wrinkles don't hurt.

3) Families are like fudge...mostly sweet, with a few nuts.

4) Today's mighty oak is just yesterday's nut that held its ground.

5) Laughing is good exercise.. It's like jogging on the inside.

6) Middle age is when you choose your cereal for the fiber, not the toy.

GREAT TRUTHS ABOUT GROWING OLD

1) Growing old is mandatory; growing up is optional.

2) Forget the health food. I need all the preservatives I can get.

3) When you fall down, you wonder what else you can do while you're down there.

4) You're getting old when you get the same sensation from a rocking chair that you once got from a roller coaster.

5) It's frustrating when you k now all the answers but nobody bothers to ask you the questions.

6) Time may be a great healer, but it's a lousy beautician.

7) Wisdom comes with age, but sometimes age comes alone.

THE FOUR STAGES OF LIFE:

1) You believe in Santa Claus.

2) You don't believe in Santa Claus.

3) You are Santa Claus.

4) You look like Santa Claus.

SUCCESS:

At age 4 success is. .. . Not piddling in your pants.

At age 12 success is. .. Having friends.

At age 17 success is.. Having a driver's license.

At age 35 success is. ... Having money.

At age 50 success is. .. Having money.

At age 70 success is. .. Having a driver's license.

At age 75 success is. .... Having friends.

At age 80 success is. .. Not piddling in your pants.

****

a man is driving along a highway and sees a rabbit jump out across the middle of the road.

He swerves to avoid hitting it, but unfortunately the rabbit jumps right in front of the car.

The driver, a sensitive man as well as an animal lover, pulls over and gets out to see

What has become of the rabbit? Much to his dismay, the rabbit is the Easter Bunny, and

He is DEAD *the driver feels so awful that he begins to cry. A beautiful blonde woman driving down the highway sees a man crying on the side of the road, and pulls over.*

She steps out of the car and asks the man what's wrong.

"I feel terrible,"! He explains, "I accidentally hit the Easter Bunny with my car and KILLED HIM*."*

The blonde says, "Don't worry."

She runs to her car and pulls out a spray can. She walks over to the limp, dead Easter bunny, bends down, and sprays the contents onto him. The Easter Bunny jumps up, waves its paw at the two of them and hops off down the road.

Ten feet away he stops, turns around and waves again, he hops down the road another 10 feet, turns and waves, hops another ten feet, turns and waves, and repeats this again and again and again and again, until he hops out of sight.

The man is astonished. He runs over to the woman and demands, "What is in that can?

What did you spray on the Easter Bunny?"

The woman turns the can around so that the man can read the label .It says...

"Hair Spray:

Restores life to dead hair,

And adds permanent wave."

Happy Easter!!!

****

A young lady was in the maternity ward just prior to labor is asked by the midwife if she would like her husband to be present at the birth.

"I'm afraid I don't have a husband" she replies.

"OK Do you have a boyfriend?" asks the midwife.

"No, no boyfriend either."

Do you have a partner then?"

"No, I'm not attached; I'll be having my baby on my own."

After the birth the midwife again speaks to the young woman,

"You have a healthy bouncing baby girl, but I must tell you before you see her that the baby is black."

"Well," replies the girl,

"I was very down on my luck, with no money and nowhere to live, and so I accepted a job in a porn film. The lead man was black."

"Oh, I'm very sorry," says the midwife, "that's really none of my business and I'm sorry that I have to ask you these awkward questions but I must also tell you that the baby has blonde hair."

"Well yes," the girl again replies, "you see the co-star in the movie was this Swedish guy."

"Oh, I'm sorry,"

The midwife repeats, "That's really none of my business either and I hate to pry further but your baby also has slanted eyes."

"Yes," continues the girl, "there was a little Chinese man also in the movie, I really had no choice."

At this, the midwife again apologizes, collects the baby and presents her to the girl, who immediately proceeds to give the baby a slap on the butt. The baby starts crying and the mother exclaims, "Thank god for that!"

"What do you mean?" says the midwife, shocked.

"Well," says the girl extremely relieved, "I had this horrible feeling that baby was going to bark."

****

Printed by Libri Plureos GmbH in Hamburg, Germany